3/15

GED® TEST
SOCIAL STUDIES
FLASH REVIEW

Related Titles

GED® Test RLA Flash Review
GED® Test Science Flash Review
GED® Test Mathematical Reasoning Flash Review
GED® Test Power Practice

GED® TEST
SOCIAL STUDIES
FLASH REVIEW

LEARNINGEXPRESS®

NEW YORK

Cataloging-in-Publication Data is on file with the Library of Congress.

Printed in the United States of America

9 8 7 6 5 4 3 2 1

First Edition

ISBN 978-1-61103-005-01

For information on LearningExpress, other LearningExpress products, or bulk sales,
please write to us at:
    80 Broad Street
    4th Floor
    New York, NY 10004

Or visit us at:
    www.learningexpressllc.com

CONTENTS

INTRODUCTION

About the GED® Social Studies Test

The GED® test measures how well you can apply problem solving, analytical reasoning, and critical thinking skills alongside your understanding of high school–level social studies.

The test is delivered on a computer and consists of approximately 35 multiple-choice, fill-in-the-blank, drop-down, drag-and-drop, and hot-spot questions, including an extended-response question. The questions are based on relevant social studies materials, including brief texts, maps, graphics, and tables.

Many of the brief texts featured will be drawn from materials reflecting "the Great American Conversation, which includes our founding documents, such as the Declaration of Independence, as well as other documents and speeches from U.S. history that express issues and values that have shaped American actions and ideals." You'll have 90 minutes to complete the test.

The new GED® Social Studies Test assesses important ideas in two ways:

1. Every question tests a social studies "practice" skill. These skills measure the critical thinking and reasoning skills that are essential to social studies success.
2. Each question is drawn from one of the four main content areas in social studies—**Civics and Government**, **Geography and the World**, **Economics**, and **U.S. History**.

How to Use This Book

GED® Test Social Studies Flash Review is designed to help you prepare for and succeed on the official exam—a strong knowledge of core social studies concepts will get you confident and prepared for test day.

This book contains more than 600 important concepts, events, terms, ideas, and practice questions in social studies. The cards are organized by topic for easy access. It works well as a stand-alone study tool for the GED® Social Studies test, but it is recommended that it be used to supplement additional preparation for the exam.

The following are some suggestions for making the most of this effective resource as you structure your study plan:

- Do not try to review this entire book all at once. Cramming is not the most effective approach to test prep. The best approach is to build a realistic study schedule that lets you review one topic each day (refer to the Table of Contents to see where each new topic begins).
- Mark the cards that you have trouble with, so that they will be easy to return to later for further study.
- Make the most of this book's portability—take it with you for studying on car trips, between classes, while commuting, or whenever you have some free time.
- Visit the official GED® test website for additional information to help you get prepared for test day.

Best of luck on the exam—and in earning your high school equivalency credential!

ABOLITIONISM

. . . .

ABORIGINAL

. . . .

ABSOLUTE LOCATION

GED® TEST SOCIAL STUDIES FLASH REVIEW

A reform movement during the eighteenth and nineteenth centuries that advocated the end of African slavery in Europe and the Americas.

· ·

Being the first or earliest known inhabitants of a region.

· ·

The exact position of a place on Earth's surface.

ACCRETION

. . . .

ACCULTURATION

. . . .

ACID DEPOSITIONS

GED® TEST SOCIAL STUDIES FLASH REVIEW

The slow process of a sea plate sliding under a continental plate, creating debris that can cause continents to grow outward.

• •

The cultural modification of an individual, group, or people by adapting to or borrowing traits from another culture.

• •

Wet or dry airborne acids falling to Earth.

ACID RAIN

. . . .

ALLIED POWERS

. . . .

Precipitation carrying large amounts of dissolved acids that damage buildings, forests, and crops and kill wildlife.

· ·

A military coalition formed between nations in opposition to another alliance of countries. In World War I, the Allied powers included 28 nations that opposed the Central powers. In World War II, the Allied powers fought the Axis powers.

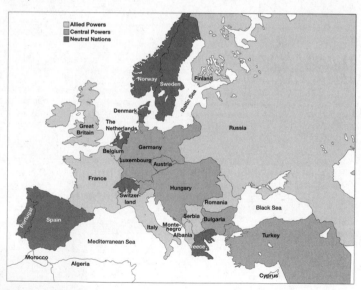

· ·

ALLUVIAL PLAIN

. . . .

ALLUVIAL SOIL

. . . .

ALTIPLANO

A floodplain, such as the Gangetic Plain in South Asia, on which flooding rivers have deposited rich soil.

· ·

Rich soil made of sand and mud deposited by running water.

· ·

Spanish for "high plain"; a region in Peru and Bolivia encircled by the Andes Mountains.

AMENDMENT

. . . .

ANIMISM

. . . .

APARTHEID

A *change* or addition to a motion, bill, written basic law, or constitution. The U.S. Constitution has 27 amendments. The first ten are collectively known as the Bill of Rights.

· ·

The belief that spirits inhabit natural objects and forces of nature.

· ·

The policy of strict separation of the races adopted in South Africa in the 1940s.

AQUACULTURE

....

AQUIFER

....

ARABLE

The cultivation of fish and other seafood.

· ·

Underground water-bearing layers of porous rock, sand, or gravel.

· ·

Suitable for growing crops.

ARCHIPELAGO

....

ARCTIC ZONE

....

ARTESIAN WELL

A group or chain of islands.

· ·

The climatic zone near the North and South Poles characterized by long, cold winters and short, cool summers.

· ·

A bored well from which water flows up like a fountain.

ARTICLES OF CONFEDERATION

. . . .

ASIA-PACIFIC ECONOMIC COOPERATION (APEC)

. . . .

ASSOCIATION OF SOUTHEAST ASIAN NATIONS (ASEAN)

The first compact (agreement) uniting the American colonies; it was formally ratified by all 13 states in 1781. It was replaced by the U.S. Constitution in 1789.

. . . .

A trade group whose members ensure that trade among the member countries of Asia and the Pacific is efficient and fair.

. . . .

An organization formed in 1967 to promote regional development and trade in Southeast Asia.

ATHEISM

. . . .

ATMOSPHERE

. . . .

ATOLL

The belief that there is no God.

· ·

A layer of gases surrounding Earth.

· ·

A ring-shaped island formed by coral building up along the rim of an underwater volcano, usually with a central lagoon.

GED® TEST SOCIAL STUDIES FLASH REVIEW

AUTOCRACY

....

AUTONOMOUS AREAS

....

AVALANCHE

A government in which one person rules with unlimited power and authority.

· ·

Minor political subunits created in the former Soviet Union and designed to recognize the special status of minority groups within existing republics.

· ·

A large mass of ice, snow, or rock that slides down a mountainside.

AXIS

. . . .

BALKANIZE

. . . .

BARTERING

An imaginary line that runs through the center of the earth between the North and South Poles.

· ·

To divide a region into smaller regions, often hostile toward each other.

· ·

As communities grew, a system of bartering—trading goods or services—developed.

BILL OF RIGHTS

. . . .

BOLSHEVIK

. . . .

BOSTON TEA PARTY

The first ten amendments to the U.S. Constitution. Ratified in 1791, the Bill of Rights safeguards the liberties of individuals. These liberties include:

- the right to practice one's religion freely
- the right to free speech
- the right to a free press
- the right to bear firearms
- the right to meet and to petition the government
- the right to a fair and speedy trial
- the right to representation by a lawyer
- the right to know the crime with which one is being charged
- protection from being tried twice for the same crime
- protection from excessive bail and/or cruel and unusual punishment

• •

A member of the radical faction of the Russian socialist party that took power in Russia and formed the Communist Party in 1918.

• •

A 1773 incident staged by American colonists protesting the British tax on tea. The colonists threw three shipments of tea into Boston Harbor.

BUBONIC PLAGUE

. . . .

BUSINESS CYCLE

. . . .

CAPITALISM

An infectious disease that killed up to one-third of all Europeans in the fourteenth century. Also called "the Black Death."

· ·

A period of low productivity followed by a period of high productivity in a capitalist economy.

· ·

An economic system in which individuals and private organizations produce and distribute goods and services in a free market.

Characteristics	Examples
• Individuals and private organizations own and operate businesses. • Free market determines production and distribution of goods and services. • Prices set by supply and demand.	• United States • Sweden • Australia

GED® TEST SOCIAL STUDIES FLASH REVIEW

CENTRAL POWERS

. . . .

CHARTER

. . . .

A military coalition of nations that fought against the Allied powers in World War I. The Central powers included Austria-Hungary, Germany, Bulgaria, and Turkey.

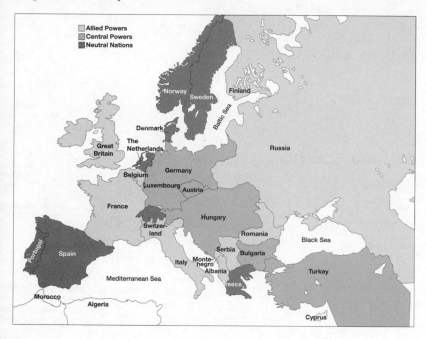

A text or document that provides specific rights to a group or person, often issued by a government.

CHECKS AND BALANCES

. . . .

CIVILIZATION

. . . .

CLIMACTIC ZONE

GED® TEST SOCIAL STUDIES FLASH REVIEW

A system outlined by the U.S. Constitution that divides authority between the executive, legislative, and judicial branches of the federal government so that no branch of government dominates the others.

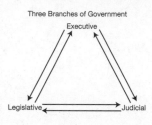

Three Branches of Government

Executive

Legislative — Judicial

· ·

An advanced state of intellectual, cultural, and technological development in human society.

· ·

Any of several broad areas that lie along latitudinal lines between the equator and the North and South Poles.

CLIMATE

....

COLD WAR

....

COMMISSION

The atmospheric characteristics near the Earth's surface over a period of time. Climate includes average temperature, rainfall, humidity, wind, and barometric pressure.

· ·

Term for the post–World War II rivalry between the United States and the Union of Soviet Socialist Republics (USSR) that ended in 1989.

· ·

A form of local government in which voters elect commissioners to head a city or county department, such as the fire, police, or public works department.

COMMUNISM

· ·

COMMUNIST MANIFESTO

· ·

An economic and political system in which the means of production are owned collectively and controlled by the state.

Characteristics	Examples
• State, or the community, owns *all* businesses. • State controls distribution of goods and services. • State provides social services.	• People's Republic of China • Cuba • Former Soviet Union

. . . .

A document of communist principles written by Karl Marx in 1848.

. . . .

CONFEDERATE STATES OF AMERICA

. . . .

A republic formed in 1861 by 11 Southern states that withdrew from the United States. After its 1865 defeat in the American Civil War, the republic dissolved.

Free States

California	New Hampshire
Connecticut	New Jersey
Illinois	New York
Indiana	Ohio
Iowa	Oregon
Kansas	Pennsylvania
Maine	Rhode Island
Massachusetts	Vermont
Michigan	Wisconsin
Minnesota	

Slave States

Alabama*	Mississippi*
Arkansas*	Missouri
Delaware	North Carolina*
Florida*	South Carolina*
Georgia*	Tennessee*
Kentucky	Texas*
Louisiana*	Virginia*
Maryland	

Territories

Colorado	Nevada
Dakota	New Mexico
Indian	Utah
Nebraska	Washington

*Confederate States

CONSTITUTION

....

CONSTITUTION OF THE UNITED STATES

....

CONSUMER PRICE INDEX (CPI)

The fundamental principles of a nation's government embodied in one document or several documents.

• •

The fundamental laws of the United States, written in 1787 and ratified in 1788.

• •

A measure of change in the cost of common goods and services, such as food, clothing, rent, fuel, and others.

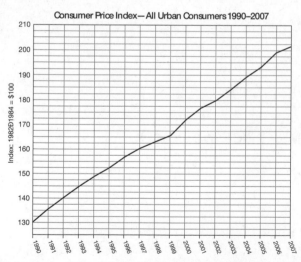

Consumer Price Index—All Urban Consumers 1990–2007

The graph shows the CPI in all U.S. cities between 1990 and 2007. To make comparisons between years, the graph uses the years 1982–1984 as a base period (1982–1984 = $100). For instance, if the average urban consumer spent $100 on living expenses in 1982–1984, he or she spent more than $150 on the same expenses in 1995.

CONTINENTAL CONGRESS

. . . .

CONTINENTAL DRIFT

. . . .

COST OF LIVING

An assembly of delegates from the American colonies who served as a governmental body that directed the war for independence.

• •

The region on a continent where new crust is being created and the plates on either side of the rift are moving apart.

• •

The price of common goods and services that are considered living expenses, such as food, clothing, rent, fuel, and others.

COUNCIL-MANAGER

· ·

CRUSADES

· ·

CULTURAL GEOGRAPHY

A form of local government in which voters elect council members, who, in turn, hire a manager to run the day-to-day operations of the locality.

· ·

Any of the military campaigns led by European Christians during the Middle Ages to recover the Holy Land from Muslims.

· ·

The study of the relationship between humans and their physical environment.

CULTURE

. . . .

DECLARATION OF INDEPENDENCE

. . . .

DEFLATION

A shared way of living among a group of people that develops over time.

· ·

A document adopted on July 4, 1776, in which the American colonies proclaimed their independence from Great Britain.

· ·

A decrease in prices due to decreased money supply and an increased quantity of consumer goods.

DEMAND

. . . .

DEMOCRACY

. . . .

DEMOGRAPHY

The quantity of goods or services that consumers want to buy at any given price. According to the principle of demand, demand decreases as price increases and vice versa.

• •

A form of government in which decisions are made by the people, either directly or through elected representatives.

Characteristics	Examples
• In *representative democracy*, people elect officials to represent their views. • In *direct democracy*, decisions are made by the people.	*Representative:* • United States • Canada • Most European nations *Direct:* • Switzerland

• •

The study of changes in population through birth rate, death rate, migration, and other factors.

DICTATORSHIP

. . . .

DIRECT ELECTION

. . . .

DISCOUNT RATE

A form of government in which one ruler has absolute power over many aspects of society, including social, economic, and political life.

Characteristics	Examples
• It is ruled by one leader who has absolute power over many aspects of life, including social, economic, and political. • Leader is not elected by the people.	• Nazi (National Socialist) government of Adolf Hitler • General Augusto Pinochet in Chile from 1973 to 1990 • North Korea

· ·

A type of electoral process in which the citizens of a state or country elect the government officials and representatives.

· ·

The interest rate that the U.S. Federal Reserve Board charges banks to borrow money.

DRED SCOTT DECISION

....

ELECTORAL COLLEGE

....

ENLIGHTENMENT

An 1857 U.S. Supreme Court decision that ruled that the Court could not ban citizens from bringing slaves into free territories.

. . . .

The system by which the president of the United States is elected, wherein the electors of each state cast their electoral votes for the winner of the popular vote in their state.

Currently, a presidential candidate needs 270 electoral votes to win the election.

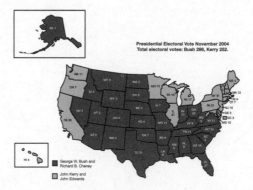

The electoral college is a group of electors who choose the president and vice president. Each state is allowed the same number of electors as its total number of U.S. senators and representatives—so each state has at least three electors. In most states, the candidate who wins the most popular votes earns that state's electoral votes.

Source: National Archives and Records Administration

. . . .

A philosophical movement of the eighteenth century in Europe and North America that emphasized rational thought.

EQUILIBRIUM (ECONOMICS)

....

EXECUTIVE BRANCH

....

FASCISM

When supply of a good or service equals that which customers are willing to buy (demand).

· ·

The arm of government that carries out laws.

Members	Characteristics
• President • Vice President • Agencies • Departments	• A president is elected by the voters for a four-year term. • A president cannot serve more than two terms. • The vice president becomes head of state if the president becomes disabled or dies in office. • Agencies carry out a president's policies and provide special services. • Department heads advise a president and carry out policies.

· ·

An Italian term for a military-based totalitarian government.

GED® TEST SOCIAL STUDIES FLASH REVIEW

FEDERAL RESERVE SYSTEM (THE FED)

. . . .

FEDERALISM

. . . .

FEDERALIST PAPERS

GED® TEST SOCIAL STUDIES FLASH REVIEW

U.S. banking system established in 1913. Includes 12 Federal Reserve banks under an eight-member controlling board.

· ·

A government structure that divides power between a central government and regional governments. The United States is a federal republic, a democracy that divides power between federal, state, and local governments.

· ·

A series of 85 essays written in 1787–1788 by Alexander Hamilton, James Madison, and John Jay in which they argued that federalism would offer a government structure that would preserve the rights of states and secure individual freedoms.

FEUDALISM

. . . .

FREE ENTERPRISE

. . . .

FRENCH AND INDIAN WAR

A political and economic system that existed in Europe between the ninth and fifteenth centuries in which a lord granted land and employment to a tenant in exchange for political and military services.

· ·

Freedom of private business to organize and operate for profit with no or little government intervention.

· ·

The last of four North American wars fought between Great Britain and France in which each country fought for control of the continent (1754–1763).

GENERAL ELECTION

. . . .

GLOBAL ECONOMY

. . . .

GLOBALIZATION

An election in which the citizens of a nation or region vote to elect the ultimate winner of a political contest.

· ·

The merging of resource management systems so countries are interconnected and dependent on one another for goods and services.

· ·

The increasing interconnectedness of people and places throughout the world through converging processes of economic, political, and cultural change.

GED® TEST SOCIAL STUDIES FLASH REVIEW

GOVERNMENT

. . . .

GREAT DEPRESSION

. . . .

GROSS DOMESTIC PRODUCT (GDP)

The act or process of governing; the control of public policy within a political organization.

· ·

A severe economic recession characterized by bank closings, failed businesses, high unemployment, and homelessness that lasted through the 1930s in the United States.

· ·

A measure of the total value of goods and services produced within a nation over the course of a year.

GROSS NATIONAL PRODUCT (GNP)

· ·

HEMISPHERE

· ·

HIROSHIMA

GED® TEST SOCIAL STUDIES FLASH REVIEW

A measure of the value of goods and services produced within a nation as well as its foreign investments over the course of a year.

· ·

Half of a sphere or globe, as in Earth's Northern and Southern Hemispheres.

· ·

A city in southwestern Japan that was the target in August 1945 of the first atomic bomb ever dropped on a populated area.

HOLOCAUST

. . . .

HUMANISM

. . . .

HYDROELECTRIC POWER

GED® TEST SOCIAL STUDIES FLASH REVIEW

Persecution and murder of millions of Jewish people and other Europeans under Adolf Hitler's Nazi regime.

. . . .

A cultural and intellectual movement of the Renaissance that emphasized classical ideals as a result of a rediscovery of ancient Greek and Roman literature and art.

. . . .

Electrical energy generated by falling water.

HYDROSPHERE

....

IDEOLOGY

....

IMMIGRATION

The watery areas of the earth, including oceans, lakes, rivers, and other bodies of water.

· ·

Ideas or characteristics of a person, group, or political party.

· ·

The process of moving and settling in a country or region to which one is not native.

IMPERIALISM

. . . .

INDUSTRIALIZATION

. . . .

INDUSTRIAL REVOLUTION

The practice of extending a nation's power by territorial acquisition or by economic and political influence over other nations.

· ·

The transition from an agricultural society to one based on industry or manufacturing.

· ·

The extensive social and economic changes brought about by the shift from the manufacturing of goods by hand to large-scale factory production that began in England in the late eighteenth century.

GED® TEST SOCIAL STUDIES FLASH REVIEW

INFLATION

. . . .

INTOLERABLE ACTS

. . . .

ISOLATIONISM

GED® TEST SOCIAL STUDIES FLASH REVIEW

An increase in prices due to an increase in the amount of money in circulation and a decreased supply of consumer goods.

· ·

A series of laws passed by the British Parliament in 1774 to punish the colony of Massachusetts for the Boston Tea Party.

· ·

A national policy of avoiding political alliances with other nations.

GED® TEST SOCIAL STUDIES FLASH REVIEW

JUDICIAL BRANCH

· ·

JUDICIAL REVIEW

· ·

LABOR MARKET

The arm of government that interprets laws.

Members	Characteristics
• U.S. Supreme Court • Circuit Courts of Appeals • Federal District Courts	• U.S. Supreme Court is the highest court in the nation. • The president appoints the nine justices of the Supreme Court. • Term is for life.

. . . .

A doctrine that allows the U.S. Supreme Court to invalidate laws and executive actions if the Court decides they conflict with the Constitution. This power was not established until the 1803 case of *Marbury v. Madison.*

. . . .

The market in which workers compete for jobs and employers compete for workers. As in other markets, the labor market is driven by supply and demand.

LABOR UNION

· ·

LAISSEZ-FAIRE

· ·

LEGEND

An organization of wage earners that uses group action to seek better economic and working conditions.

· ·

A doctrine that believes economic systems work better without intervention by government.

· ·

A table or list that explains the symbols used on a map or chart.

LEGISLATIVE BRANCH

....

LONGITUDE

....

LOUISIANA PURCHASE

The law-making arm of a government.

Members	Characteristics

• U.S. Congress:
  • House of Representatives
  • Senate
	• Number of representatives for each state is based on the population of that state.
	• Representatives serve two-year terms.
	• Each state has two senators.
	• Senators serve six-year terms.

· ·

The distance measured by degrees or time east or west from the prime meridian.

· ·

The vast land area in North America bought by the United States from France in 1803.

MANTLE

....

MARKET

....

MARKET ECONOMY

The thick middle layer of Earth's interior structure, consisting of dense, hot rock.

· ·

Any forum in which an exchange between buyers and sellers takes place.

· ·

An economic system based on free enterprise; businesses are privately owned, and production and prices are determined by supply and demand.

GED® TEST SOCIAL STUDIES FLASH REVIEW

MARTIAL LAW

....

MAYFLOWER COMPACT

....

MAYOR COUNCIL

The control and policing of civilians by military rules.

· ·

An agreement which stated that the settlers of the Plymouth Colony would make decisions by the will of the majority. It was the first instance of self-government in America.

· ·

A form of local government in which voters elect a mayor as city or town executive and elect a council member from each ward.

MEGALOPOLIS

. . . .

METROPOLITAN AREA

. . . .

MIDDLE AGES

A thickly populated area centered around several large and small cities or one large city.

· ·

The region that includes a central city and its surrounding suburbs.

· ·

A period in Europe beginning with the decline of the Roman Empire in the fifth century and ending with the Renaissance in 1453.

GED® TEST SOCIAL STUDIES FLASH REVIEW

MIGRATION

· ·

MIXED ECONOMY

· ·

MONARCHY

The movement of people from place to place.

. . . .

A system of resource management in which the government supports and regulates enterprise through decisions that affect the marketplace.

. . . .

A form of government headed by one ruler who claims power through hereditary or divine right.

Characteristics	Examples
• One person from a royal family is ruler. • Power is inherited from generation to generation. • Absolute monarchs have complete authority. • *Constitutional monarchs* have limited authority; a representative democracy governs.	*Absolute monarchy:* • Swaziland • Saudi Arabia *Constitutional monarchy:* • Great Britain • Japan • Sweden • Morocco

MONOPOLY

....

MONOTHEISM

....

MONSOON

A situation in which a specific person or enterprise owns all or nearly all of the market for a particular commodity. A monopoly is characterized by a lack of viable economic competition to produce a good or service. Because losing customers to competitors is not an issue, the specific person or enterprise can set a price that is significantly higher than the cost of producing the good or service.

· ·

The worship or belief in a single God. Monotheistic religious systems include Christianity, Judaism, Islam, and Sikhism.

Religion	Origin	Characteristics
Judaism	Middle East, now Israel—the Jewish calendar begins with the biblical time of the Creation	• The belief in a single, all-powerful God is central to Judaism. • The Torah—the instructions believed to be handed down from God to Moses—encompasses Jewish law and custom.
Christianity	Jerusalem, now in Israel—Christian calendar begins with the birth of Jesus	• Early followers believed that Jesus fulfilled the Jewish prophesy of the Messiah. • The Gospels in the Bible's New Testament describe the teachings and life of Jesus. • Beliefs include that Jesus is the son of God and that after crucifixion, he rose from the dead.
Islam	Arabia in 622 A.D.	• Its followers, called Muslims, believe in one all-powerful God. • Muslims adhere to the codes of living set forth in the holy book of Islam, the Qur'an (Koran). • The founder of Islam was Muhammed, a prophet who lived in Mecca in the sixth century, A.D.

· ·

In Asia, seasonal wind that brings warm, moist air from the oceans in summer and cold, dry air from inland in winter.

MUTUALISM

. . . .

NAGASAKI

. . . .

NATIONALISM

A class of relationship between two organisms in which both organisms benefit. The pollination process involving flowering plants and insects (such as bees and wasps) is the best example of this. While the insects get their food in the form of nectar from the plants, the plants benefit from pollination carried out by these insects, which helps them reproduce.

. . . .

A seaport in western Japan that was the target in August 1945 of the second atomic bomb ever dropped on a populated area. The bombing marked the end of World War II.

. . . .

The belief in the right of each people to be an independent nation.

NATURAL BOUNDARY

....

NATURAL INCREASE

....

NATURAL RESOURCES

A fixed limit or extent defined along physical geographic features like mountains and rivers.

. . . .

The growth rate of a population.

. . . .

Substances from the earth that are not man-made.

NATURALIZATION

....

NEW DEAL

....

NOMAD

The process by which one becomes a citizen of a new country.

· ·

A domestic reform program initiated by the administration of President Franklin D. Roosevelt to provide relief and recovery from the Great Depression.

The New Deal
Agricultural Adjustment Act—paid farmers to slow their production in order to stabilize food prices
National Industrial Recovery Act—outlined codes for fair competition in industry
Securities and Exchange Commission—established to regulate stock market
Federal Deposit Insurance Corporation—insured bank deposits in the case that banks fail
Public Works Administration—built roads, public buildings, dams
Tennessee Valley Authority—brought electric power to parts of the Southeast

· ·

A member of a wandering pastoral people.

NORTH AMERICAN FREE TRADE AGREEMENT (NAFTA)

....

NUCLEAR PROLIFERATION

....

OLIGARCHY

The trade pact made in 1994 by Canada, the United States, and Mexico.

· ·

The spreading development of nuclear arms.

· ·

A form of government in which decisions are made by a small, elite group that is not elected by the people.

Characteristics	Examples
• It is governed by a small upper-class group. • Leaders are not elected by the general populace.	• City-state of Sparta in ancient Greece • Apartheid-era South Africa

OUTSOURCING

....

OZONE LAYER

....

PARLIAMENT

The practice of subcontracting manufacturing work to outside companies, especially foreign or nonunion companies.

· ·

The atmospheric layer with protective gases that prevents solar rays from reaching Earth's surface.

· ·

A national legislative body made up of elected and sometimes non-elected officials. The British Parliament is made up of the House of Commons and the House of Lords.

PASTORALISM

....

PEARL HARBOR

....

PHYSICAL MAP

The raising of livestock.

· ·

A United States military base in the Pacific Ocean that was attacked by Japan in 1941. The attack led to the entry of the United States into World War II.

· ·

A map that shows the location of natural features such as mountains and rivers; can also show cities and countries.

GED® TEST SOCIAL STUDIES FLASH REVIEW

PILGRIMS

. . . .

PLURALITY SYSTEM

. . . .

PLYMOUTH COLONY

GED® TEST SOCIAL STUDIES FLASH REVIEW

A group of religious separatists who were the founders of the Plymouth Colony on the coast of Massachusetts in 1620.

· ·

An electoral system in which a candidate need only receive more votes than each of his or her opponents to win.

· ·

A settlement made by Pilgrims on the coast of Massachusetts in 1620.

GED® TEST SOCIAL STUDIES FLASH REVIEW

POLITICAL MAP

· ·

POLITICAL PARTY

· ·

POLYTHEISM

GED® TEST SOCIAL STUDIES FLASH REVIEW

A map that shows the boundaries and locations of political units such as countries, states, counties, cities, and towns.

. . . .

An organization that presents its positions on public issues and promotes candidates that support its point of view. Political parties serve several functions:

- recruit candidates and run election campaigns
- formulate positions on issues that affect the public and propose solutions
- educate the public on issues
- mobilize their members to vote
- create voting blocs in Congress

. . . .

The worship or belief in many Gods. Polytheistic religious systems include Buddhism, Hinduism, and Shintoism.

Religion	Origin	Characteristics
Hinduism	India in 1500 B.C.	• Hinduism has no single founder; it developed over a period of 4,000 years. • One of its main features is a caste system, in which people are born into a prescribed class and follow the ways of that class.
Buddhism	India in 525 B.C.	• It was founded by Siddhartha Gautama, called the Buddha. • Buddhists believe in a cycle of rebirth. • The ultimate goal of the Buddhist path is to achieve nirvana, an enlightened state free from suffering.

POPULATION

· ·

POSTINDUSTRIAL

· ·

PRIMARY ELECTION

The size, makeup, and distribution of people in a given area.

· ·

Refers to an economy with less emphasis on heavy industry and manufacturing and more emphasis on services and technology.

· ·

A preliminary contest in which voters give their preference for a political party's candidate for public office.

PRIME MERIDIAN

· ·

PRIVATIZATION

· ·

PROGRESSIVISM

GED® TEST SOCIAL STUDIES FLASH REVIEW

The meridian of 0 degrees longitude from which other longitudes are calculated.

· ·

A change to private ownership of state-owned companies and industries.

· ·

A reform movement of the early twentieth century that sought to remedy the problems created by industrialization.

PURITANS

. . . .

RATIFY

. . . .

RECESSION

A group of English migrants who sought to purify the Church of England. The group started settlements in New England in the seventeenth century.

· ·

To confirm or give formal approval to something, such as an agreement between nations.

· ·

A period of low economic productivity and income.

RECONSTRUCTION

. . . .

REFUGEE

. . . .

REGION

From 1865 to 1877, the period of readjustment and rebuilding of the South that followed the American Civil War.

· ·

One who flees his or her home for safety.

· ·

A land area that shares cultural, political, or geographic attributes that distinguish it from other areas.

RENAISSANCE

....

REPARATION

....

REPEAL

A term meaning "rebirth" that refers to a series of cultural and literary developments in Europe in the fourteenth, fifteenth, and sixteenth centuries.

. . . .

A payment for damages. An example of this is the reparations made by Germany to the Allied countries following World War I.

. . . .

To take back or undo, typically referring to the repeal of an amendment to the U.S. Constitution.

REPUBLIC

....

RESERVE RATIO

....

REVOLUTION

A government based on the concept that power resides with the people, who then elect officials to represent them in government.

· ·

A portion of deposits that banks, which are members of the Federal Reserve system, set aside and do not use to make loans.

· ·

A violent change in the political order and social structure of a society.

ROMANOV DYNASTY

. . . .

RULE OF LAW

. . . .

SECT

The family that ruled Russia from 1613 until the Russian Revolution in 1917.

· ·

The principle that all citizens, including functionaries of the government, must follow the law.

· ·

A subdivision within a religion that has its own distinctive beliefs and/or practices.

SECTIONALISM

. . . .

SEPARATION OF POWERS

. . . .

SEPARATISM

The attitude or actions of a region or section of a nation when it supports its own interests over those of the nation as a whole.

· ·

The practice of dividing the authority of a government between different branches to avoid an abuse of power.

· ·

The breaking away of one part of a country to create a separate, independent country.

SERF

· ·

SERVICE INDUSTRY

· ·

SHORTAGE

Laborer obliged to remain on the land where he or she worked in feudal times.

· ·

A business that provides a service instead of manufacturing goods.

· ·

When demand for a good or service is greater than that which is produced.

SOCIAL STUDIES

. . . .

SOCIALISM

. . . .

STAMP ACT

The study of how people live every day, including the exploration of humans' physical environments, cultures, political institutions, and economic conditions.

· ·

An economic system in which the state owns and controls the basic factors of production and distribution of wealth.

Characteristics	Examples
• State owns and operates many businesses and services. • Private ownership is allowed. • Citizens pay high taxes to fund state-run social services, including healthcare, food, and housing.	• No current examples, though many EU countries have socialist aspects.

· ·

A measure passed by the British Parliament in 1765 as a means of collecting taxes in the American colonies. It required that all printed materials, including legal documents and newspapers, carry a tax stamp.

STOCK EXCHANGE

· ·

STOCK MARKET CRASH OF 1929

· ·

SUBSISTENCE AGRICULTURE

An organized market for buying and selling stocks.

· ·

A collapse in the value of stocks that marked the onset of the Great Depression in the United States.

· ·

Farming that produces only enough crops or animal products to support a farm family's needs. Usually little is sold at local or regional markets.

SUFFRAGE

....

SUPPLY

....

SURPLUS

The right to vote.

· ·

The amount of goods and services available for purchase.

· ·

When the supply of a good or service is greater than that which customers are willing to buy (demand).

GED® TEST SOCIAL STUDIES FLASH REVIEW

SUSTAINABLE DEVELOPMENT

. . . .

TARIFF

. . . .

TOPOGRAPHY

Technological and economic growth that does not deplete the human and natural resources of a given area.

· ·

A tax on imported, and sometimes exported, goods.

· ·

The representation of features of land surfaces, including the shape and elevation of terrain, primarily through mapping.

TOTAL COST

. . . .

TOTALITARIANISM

. . . .

TOWNSHEND ACTS

GED® TEST SOCIAL STUDIES FLASH REVIEW

Total cost = number of units × price per unit.

. . . .

A government in which the rulers of the state control all aspects of society, including economic, political, cultural, intellectual, and spiritual life.

. . . .

Measures passed by British Parliament in 1767 that taxed American colonists for imported glass, lead, paints, paper, and tea.

TREATY

· ·

TREATY OF VERSAILLES

· ·

TROPIC OF CANCER

A formal agreement between sovereign nations or groups of nations.

. . . .

The major treaty of five peace treaties that ended World War I in 1919.

. . . .

An imaginary line at 23.5° north latitude.

TROPIC OF CAPRICORN

· ·

UNEMPLOYMENT

· ·

URBANIZATION

An imaginary line at 23.5° south latitude.

· ·

When willing and able wage earners cannot find jobs. The unemployment rate serves as one index of a nation's economic activity.

· ·

The movement of a population from rural areas to cities with the result of urban growth.

VETO

....

The power of the executive to block the laws passed by the legislative branch.

• •

The idea of self-government is in the first three words of the Constitution. What are these words?

. . . .

In *The Politics*, the Greek philosopher Aristotle wrote that, "Even when laws have been written down, they should not always remain unaltered." What fundamental element of the U.S. Constitution supports this idea?

a. checks and balances
b. separation of powers
c. amendment process
d. federalism

. . . .

"From each according to his ability, to each according to his need" is a slogan most associated with what form of government?

a. communism
b. democracy
c. fascism
d. monarchy

Answer: We the People

. . . .

Answer: c. An alteration, like an amendment, is a change. A constitution lays down the basic laws or rules of an organization, and amendments are changes to these rules.

. . . .

Answer: a. Communism sought a classless society based on this Marxist principle.

The following question is based on the First Amendment to the U.S. Constitution.

Congress shall make no law respecting an establishment of religion, or prohibiting the free exercise thereof; or abridging the freedom of speech or of the press; or the right of the people peaceably to assemble, and to petition the government for a redress of grievances.

—First Amendment to the U.S. Constitution

In interpreting the First Amendment, the Supreme Court has ruled that individual freedom must be weighed against the safety of the public and the rights of other citizens. Thus, the First Amendment does not protect actions that put others in danger. Which of the following actions is covered by the First Amendment according to the interpretation of the U.S. Supreme Court?

a. assembling in the middle of a street without a permit

b. falsely yelling "fire" in a crowded movie theatre

c. petitioning to impeach the president

d. engaging in human sacrifice as a religious practice

. . . .

What role do third parties such as the Populist Party play in American politics?

a. They provide continuity in times of change.

b. They provide a platform to propose new ideas and policies.

c. They regularly replace the two major parties.

d. They tend to attract important politicians from the two major parties.

. . . .

What is an amendment?

Answer: c. The right to petition is exactly the kind of political speech that the First Amendment has always protected.

. . . .

Answer: b. In U.S. history, third parties rarely have electoral success but often find their principles adopted by the major parties.

. . . .

Answer: A change or an addition (to the Constitution).

What do we call the first ten amendments to the Constitution?

· ·

Use the excerpts from the Articles of Confederation to answer the following two questions.

Articles of Confederation and Perpetual Union

between the States of New Hampshire, Massachusetts Bay, Rhode Island and Providence Plantations, Connecticut, New York, New Jersey, Pennsylvania, Delaware, Maryland, Virginia, North Carolina, South Carolina, and Georgia.

Article 1. The style of this confederacy shall be, "The United States of America."

Art. 2. Each state retains its sovereignty, freedom and independence, and every power, jurisdiction and right, which is not by this Confederation expressly delegated to the United States, in Congress assembled.

Art. 3. The said States hereby severally enter into a firm league of friendship with each other, for their common defense, the security of their liberties, and their mutual and general welfare, binding themselves to assist each other against all force offered to, or attacks made upon them, or any of them, on account of religion, sovereignty, trade, or any other pretence whatever. . . .

July 9, 1778

———————————

Based on these excerpts, the government defined by the Articles of Confederation can best be described as a
a. **business arrangement.**
b. **constitutional monarchy.**
c. **loose affiliation.**
d. **military power.**

· ·

Answer: The Bill of Rights

· ·

—————————

Answer: b. The Articles of Confederation established a "firm league of friendship" in which "each state retains its sovereignty."

· ·

What was a main difference between the U.S. Constitution and the Articles of Confederation?
a. The U.S. Constitution created new state boundaries.
b. The U.S. Constitution established a representational government.
c. The U.S. Constitution encouraged states to work together in times of war.
d. The U.S. Constitution strengthened the power of the central government.

. . . .

How many amendments does the Constitution have?

. . . .

What did the Declaration of Independence do?

Answer: d. The Constitution was established to remedy the weaknesses of the Articles of Confederation and gave more power to the central government.

· ·

Answer: Twenty-seven (27)

· ·

Answer: Announced (or declared) our independence (from Great Britain).

What is the economic system in the United States?

. . . .

Read the passage and answer the question that follows.

In 1832, Congress passed a bill to re-charter the national bank. President Andrew Jackson vetoed the bill. Henry Clay, a U.S. Senator from Kentucky, said the following about the president's veto:

"A bill to re-charter the bank, has recently passed Congress, after much deliberation, . . . the president has rejected the bill. . . .

"The veto is an extraordinary power, which, though tolerated by the Constitution, was not expected, by the convention, to be used in ordinary cases. It was designed for instances of precipitate legislation, in unguarded moments. Thus restricted, and it has been thus restricted by all former presidents, it might not be mischievous. . . .

"The veto is hardly reconcilable with the genius of representative government. It is totally irreconcilable with it, if it is to be frequently employed in respect to the expediency of measures, as well as their constitutionality. It is a feature of our government, borrowed from a prerogative of the British king. And it is remarkable, that in England it has grown obsolete, not having been used for upward of a century. . . . It can not be imagined that the Convention contemplated the application of the veto, to a question which has been so long, so often, and so thoroughly scrutinized, as that of the bank of the United States."

—Henry Clay

_____

Henry Clay expresses concerns with all of the following except
a. checks and balances.
b. federalism.
c. the power of the president.
d. the role of Congress.

. . . .

Answer: Capitalist economy or market economy

· ·

Answer: b. Only federalism, the relationship between the state and national government, is not covered in this address. This was a major concern of Henry Clay's, but he does not deal with it here.

· ·

Read the passage and answer the question that follows.

"The person of the king is sacred, and to attack him in any way is an attack on religion itself. God has the kings anointed by his prophets . . . in the same way he has bishops and altars anointed. . . . The respect given to a king is religious in nature. Serving God and respecting kings are bound together. . . ."

—Jacques Bossuet, French theologian, *Politics Drawn from the Very Words of Holy Scripture*, 1707

Based on this excerpt, Bossuet believed in
a. **unlimited monarchy.**
b. **the divine power of prophets.**
c. **the importance of religious feeling.**
d. **the separation of church and state.**

What is the "rule of law"?

Name one branch or part of the government.

_____

Answer: a. Although the word *monarchy* never appears in the quotation, Bossuet is stating the theory of the divine right of kings. By linking them with God, Bossuet believes a king's power is unlimited.

· ·

Answer: Some possible responses:

- Everyone must follow the law.
- Leaders must obey the law.
- Government must obey the law.
- No one is above the law.

· ·

Answer: Some possible responses:

- congress
- legislative
- president
- executive
- the courts
- judicial

What stops one branch of government from becoming too powerful?

. . . .

Use the table to answer the following four questions.

Voter Turnout in National Elections 1990–2012			
Year	Voting-age population	Voter turnout	Turnout of voting-age population (percent)
2012	240,926,957	130,234,600	53.6
2010	235,809,266	90,682,968	37.8
2008	231,229,580	132,618,580	56.8
2006	220,600,000	80,588,000	37.1
2004	221,256,931	122,294,978	55.3
2002	215,473,000	79,830,119	37.0
2000	205,815,000	105,586,274	51.3
1998	200,929,000	73,117,022	36.4
1996	196,511,000	96,456,345	49.1
1994	193,650,000	75,105,860	38.8
1992	189,529,000	104,405,155	55.1
1990	185,812,000	67,859,189	36.5

In which year was voter turnout highest in terms of percentage of the voting-age population?
a. 2012
b. 2008
c. 2004
d. 2000

. . . .

Answer: Checks and balances or separation of powers

• •

Answer: b. The fourth column of the table shows voter turnout as a percentage of the voting-age population. According to the table, that percentage was highest in 2008.

• •

Suppose you were deciding how many ballots to print for the 2014 election. Based on the pattern shown, how many ballots do you think you would need?
a. the same number as for 2012
b. about twice as many as for 2012
c. about half as many as for 2012
d. about three-quarters as many as for 2012

. . . .

How does the change in voter turnout between 1992 and 1994 compare with the change between 1996 and 1998?
a. In both cases, voter turnout increased by several percentage points.
b. In both cases, voter turnout declined by several percentage points.
c. In the first case, voter turnout went up; in the second, it declined.
d. In the first case, voter turnout declined; in the second, it rose.

. . . .

Which conclusion is best supported by the information in the table?
a. Turnout is higher in presidential election years.
b. Turnout declined sharply throughout the 2000s.
c. Turnout steadily increased during the 1990s and 2000s.
d. Turnout rose sharply throughout the 1990s.

Answer: d. The table shows a distinct pattern in voter turnout: in every other election, turnout goes up; then in the next election, it declines. Based on this pattern, 2012 was an "up" year and turnout will most likely decline in 2014. Furthermore, the pattern appears to be that turnout in each "down" year is about three-quarters of turnout in the preceding "up" year. Based on this pattern, for 2014 you would need to print about three-quarters as many ballots as were used in 2012.

. . . .

Answer: b. The pattern shown in the table is that in every other election, turnout goes up; then in the next election, it declines. The years 1992 and 1996 were both "up" years, followed in 1994 and 1998 by "down" years.

. . . .

Answer: a. The pattern shown in the table is that in every other election, turnout goes up; then in the next election, it declines. The "up" years, 1992, 1996, 2000, 2004, 2008, and 2012, were all presidential election years.

Who is in charge of the executive branch?

. . . .

Who makes federal laws?

. . . .

What are the two parts of the U.S. Congress?

Answer: The president of the United States

· ·

Answer: Some possible responses:

- Congress
- Senate and House of Representatives
- (U.S. or national) legislature

· ·

Answer: The Senate and House of Representatives

How many U.S. senators are there?

· ·

We elect a U.S. senator for how many years?

· ·

The House of Representatives has how many voting members?

Answer: One hundred (100)

. . . .

Answer: Six years

. . . .

Answer: Four hundred thirty-five (435)

We elect a U.S. representative for how many years?

· ·

Why do some states have more representatives than other states?

· ·

We elect a president for how many years?

Answer: Two years

· ·

Answer: Number of representatives is based on a state's population.

· ·

Answer: Four years

In what month do we vote for president?

· ·

If the president can no longer serve, who becomes
president?

· ·

If both the president and the vice president can no longer
serve, who becomes president?

Answer: November

· ·

Answer: The vice president

· ·

Answer: The Speaker of the House

Who is the commander in chief of the military?

· ·

Who signs bills to become laws?

· ·

Answer: The president of the United States

. . . .

Answer: The president of the United States

. . . .

Use the following two excerpts from the U.S. Constitution to answer the question.

The Senate of the United States shall be composed of two Senators from each state, chosen by the legislature thereof, for six years, and each Senator shall have one vote.

—U.S. Constitution, Article I, Section 3

The Senate of the United States shall be composed of two Senators from each state, elected by the people thereof, for six years; and each Senator shall have one vote. The electors in each state shall have the qualifications requisite for electors of the most numerous branch of the state legislatures.

—U.S. Constitution, Seventeenth Amendment

_____

Which statement is true based on the above information?
a. U.S. Senators have always been elected by popular vote.
b. A state's two senators can cast only one unified vote on any law.
c. The framework of the U.S. government can be altered by amendment.
d. Senators can serve only one six-year term.

. . . .

Who vetoes bills?

. . . .

What does the president's cabinet do?

Answer: c. In 1913, the Seventeenth Amendment to the U.S. Constitution took the power to elect U.S. senators from the state legislatures and gave it to the people.

. . . .

Answer: The president of the United States

. . . .

Answer: The cabinet advises the president.

If an election were held on Tuesday, November 6, in which of these states could you vote if you moved there on Monday, October 1, and registered immediately?

State	Residency Requirement
California	15-day registration requirement
Colorado	30-day residency requirement; 29-day registration requirement
Illinois	30-day residency requirement; 27-day registration requirement
Kentucky	28-day registration requirement
Missouri	No durational residency requirement; must be registered by the fourth Wednesday prior to election

a. **California only**
b. **California and Kentucky only**
c. **all the states listed except Missouri**
d. **all the states listed**

• •

What is the highest court in the United States?

• •

GED® TEST SOCIAL STUDIES FLASH REVIEW

Answer: d. None of the states in the chart has a residency requirement of more than 30 days. The time from October 1 to November 6 is more than 30 days. If the person registered immediately, the registration requirements of California and Missouri would have been met.

. . . .

Answer: The Supreme Court

. . . .

How many justices are on the Supreme Court?

. . . .

How old do citizens have to be to vote for president?

. . . .

Answer: There are nine justices on the Supreme Court.

· ·

Answer: Citizens eighteen and older can vote.

· ·

The cartoonist who drew this image is most likely hoping to elicit which of the following reactions?

Source: College Debt #106133, by Robert Englehart, *The Hartford Courant*, 2/10/2012.

a. If you can't manage your money, you need to suffer the consequences.
b. People who can't afford to go to college should not have incurred the debt in the first place.
c. Families need to spend on more practical things than a college education.
d. We need to help our college graduates who are drowning in debt.

. . . .

Answer: d. The cartoonist hopes that the reaction would be sympathy for the college grad and a desire to help; he urges sympathy in the viewer through a depiction of the just-graduated college student as being pulled under water by the heavy responsibility of student loan debt.

The amendment process to the U.S. Constitution requires that three-quarters of the states approve a proposed amendment for it to go into effect. Which of the following conclusions regarding the number of states needed to ratify an amendment is correct?

a. All the original 13 states were needed to ratify the first ten amendments since they were proposed with the Constitution and were part of a grand bargain between Federalists and Anti-Federalists.

b. Twenty-seven states were needed to ratify the Thirteenth Amendment, which abolished slavery, since there were 36 states at the end of the Civil War.

c. The reason that 36 states were needed to repeal the Eighteenth Amendment in 1933 was that 36 states were needed to ratify the Eighteenth Amendment creating Prohibition in 1919.

d. Because we now have 50 states, 37 states will have to be on record ratifying the Sixteenth Amendment—which was passed in 1909 and authorized the income tax—even though 36 states were needed then.

. . . .

One of the powers that is shared by the federal and state governments is the power to raise revenue. What was the most likely reason that led to this power being shared?

a. The federal and state governments both need money to operate effectively.

b. The federal government would be too weak without the power to raise revenue.

c. The federal government would be too strong with the power to raise revenue.

d. It helps maintain the balance of power between the two levels of government.

. . . .

Answer: b. Three-quarters of 36 states, the number of states at the end of the Civil War, is 27 states.

· ·

Answer: d. Sharing the power to raise revenue helps keep both levels of government strong and independent and maintains a balance of power.

· ·

Andover, Massachusetts, claims to be the largest community in the world to be governed by an annual Town Meeting. All registered voters are eligible to attend and vote at Town Meeting. Citizens have the opportunity to stand up and be counted on issues such as the town and school budgets and special projects and issues, such as new sidewalks and changes in the zoning laws.

The type of government in Andover is best described as
a. anarchy.
b. oligarchy.
c. dictatorship.
d. democracy.

. . . .

This question is based on the following excerpt from Article 1 of the U.S. Constitution.

Section 8. The Congress shall have power to lay and collect taxes, duties, imposts and excises, to pay the debts and provide for the common defense and general welfare of the United States; but all duties, imposts and excises shall be uniform throughout the United States. . . .

To make all laws which shall be necessary and proper for carrying into execution the foregoing powers, and all other powers vested by this Constitution in the government of the United States, or in any department or officer thereof.

—United States Constitution, Article 1, Section 8

_____

The second paragraph is sometimes known as the elastic clause. The elastic clause has been used to justify all of the following acts of Congress except
a. establish a national bank.
b. draft young people into the U.S. Army.
c. outlaw racial discrimination practices.
d. eliminate judicial review.

. . . .

Answer: d. Town Meeting, in which every registered voter can participate, is considered to be direct democracy.

· ·

_____

Answer: d. Congress cannot control the power of judicial review. This is a constitutional power given to the judicial branch. Judicial review cannot be changed (because the Constitution is the highest law) except by constitutional amendment.

· ·

The notion that a legitimate government can only function with the consent of the governed is known as popular sovereignty. Which of the following slogans from the American Revolutionary period most directly supports the notion of popular sovereignty?
a. Don't tread on me.
b. A man's house is his castle.
c. No taxation without representation.
d. Join or die.

· ·

While Iran does have an elected president and legislature, it also has a supreme leader, the Islamic cleric Ayatollah Sayyed Ali Khamenei, who was elected by the Islamic Assembly of Experts and has ruled Iran since 1989. The Supreme Leader is the highest-ranking political and religious authority in the Islamic Republic of Iran. The type of government in Iran is best described as a(n)
a. theocracy.
b. oligarchy.
c. dictatorship.
d. democracy.

· ·

Answer: c. *No taxation without representation* most directly expresses the notion of popular sovereignty. The colonists claimed that the right to collect taxes depended on the consent of the people.

. . . .

Answer: a. While having an elected Parliament and president is considered to be evidence of democracy, all democratically elected individuals can be overruled by a religious authority. A government in which the final say is given to a religious leader is a theocracy.

. . . .

Use the information below to answer the following three questions.

Presidential Veto Power

When a bill is presented to the president, he can sign it into law or he can veto the bill. Bills that are vetoed return to Congress. If a vetoed bill is passed by a two-thirds majority of both houses, it becomes law over the president's veto. If the president does not take any action, the bill becomes a law without his signature. If Congress adjourns in this time, however, the bill does not become law. This is called a pocket veto.

The chart shows the total number of vetoes in U.S. history.

Total vetoes	Regular vetoes	Pocket vetoes	Vetoes overridden	Percentage of pocket vetoes overridden	Percentage of regular vetoes overridden
2,564	1,497	1,067	110	4%	7%

How is a pocket veto different from a regular veto?
a. **A pocket veto is done in secret.**
b. **The president does not take any action.**
c. **Congress cannot overturn a pocket veto.**
d. **A pocket veto can involve just one part of a bill.**

_____

Answer: b. The president does not take any action in a pocket veto.

· ·

Which chart shows the information on the table?

a.

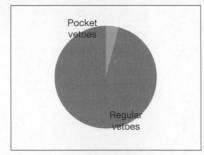

b.

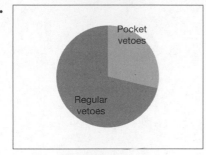

c.

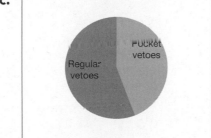

d.

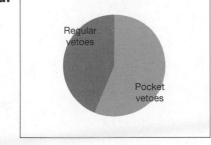

Answer: c. There were 1,067 pocket vetoes and 1,497 regular vetoes, as shown on this chart.

Which claim is supported by the information in the excerpt and the table?
a. Presidents rarely use the pocket veto.
b. Congress is better able to overturn regular vetoes than pocket vetoes.
c. Congress does not have the authority to overturn presidential vetoes.
d. Early presidents were less apt to use veto power than today's presidents.

. . . .

Read the paragraph below and answer the following two questions.

On May 26, 2009, President Barack Obama nominated Judge Sonia Sotomayor to the U.S. Supreme Court. She then met with the Senate Judiciary Committee to answer questions about her experiences. The Senate Judiciary Committee approved of Sotomayor's nomination and sent it to the Senate for a vote. The Senate approved Barack Obama's nomination by a vote of 68 to 31. Sotomayor was sworn into office on August 8, 2009, becoming the first Hispanic and the third woman to sit on the Supreme Court.

The nomination process demonstrates a check of which branch of government on the power of the other two branches?
a. legislative
b. judicial
c. executive
d. none of these

. . . .

Answer: b. Regular vetoes have been overturned 7% of the time, but the overall rate is lower, suggesting that pocket vetoes are harder to overturn. The text also suggests this, as Congress would need to be called back into session to reconsider and take a new vote on a vetoed bill.

· ·

———————

Answer: a. The nomination process demonstrates a check of the legislative branch of government on the power of the other two branches. The excerpt discusses the role that the Senate plays in the nomination of Supreme Court Justices. The Senate is part of the legislative branch. The Constitution gives the president the power to nominate a judge. The confirmation process provides the legislative branch with a check on this power.

· ·

Use the chart to answer the following two questions.

The following chart compares the most common basic forms of local government in the United States.

	Council-Manager	Mayor-Council	Commission	Town Meeting
	Most common form of government	Most common form of government among largest U.S. cities	Oldest form of government, but exists in fewer than 1% of cities	Practiced in fewer than 5% of cities; prevalent primarily in small New England towns
Legislative functions	Elected council sets policy	Elected council sets policy	Commission sets policy. Voters elect individual commissioners to small governing board	Policy is made by all voters at town meetings; in representative town meetings, representatives are elected to attend and vote on issues at town meetings
Executive functions	Council hires professional city manager to carry out day-to-day administration	Mayor is elected separately from the council; mayor may be paid position	Commission has administrative functions. Each commissioner is responsible for separate aspect of the city (e.g., fire, police, public works, etc.)	Selectmen implement policy

_____

The executive personnel and functions of which type of local government most directly mimic those of the federal government?
a. council-manager
b. mayor-council
c. commission
d. town meeting

· ·

Which conclusion can most fairly be drawn from the chart?
a. The size of a city affects the form of government that works best.
b. Once a city has selected a form of government, it is difficult to change.
c. The most democratic forms of local government are also the most common.
d. Mayor-council government works more efficiently than the city-council form.

· ·

Answer: b. This is the correct answer. Like the president, the mayor leads the executive branch and is an elected position.

Answer: a. Cities of different sizes tend to gravitate to a specific type of government. While town meetings are sometimes used in very small communities, they would likely be impractical in larger communities, which generally need a full-time executive who can take the lead on managing the complexities of a large city.

Based on the information in the excerpt, which step happens first in the Supreme Court judge approval process?

a. The Supreme Court reviews a candidate's qualifications.
b. The Senate takes a vote on the candidate.
c. The president nominates a candidate for the Supreme Court.
d. The Supreme Court nominee is sworn in.

· ·

Use the information below to answer the following three questions.

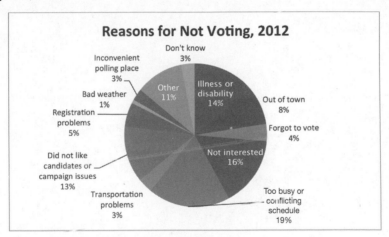

Reasons for Not Voting, 2012

What is the biggest reason that people do not vote?

a. illness or disability
b. not interested
c. too busy or conflicting schedule
d. did not like candidates or campaign issues

· ·

Answer: c. The first step in the Supreme Court judge approval process is the president nominating the candidate. He or she does not approve the nomination.

· ·

_____

Answer: c. To find the most common reason given, look for the biggest slice of the pie, or the item with the highest percentage. The most common reason given was by people who said they were too busy or had conflicting schedules, which is 19%. The next biggest reasons given were not interested (16%), illness or disability (14%), and did not like candidates or campaign issues (13%).

· ·

Which change would likely have the greatest impact on voting rates?
a. relocating polling places
b. extending the polling hours or days
c. sending reminders to registered voters
d. changing the voter registration process

· ·

Consider the following opinion: Americans are apathetic about politics and do not appreciate the right to vote.

What evidence from the chart could be used to support this opinion?
a. Sixteen percent of Americans who did not vote said it was because they were not interested.
b. Five percent of Americans who did not vote said it was because they had registration problems.
c. The most often cited reason for not voting was that Americans were too busy.
d. Thirteen percent of those who did not vote did not like the candidates or campaign issues.

· ·

Answer: b. Being too busy was cited by more nonvoters than any other reason. Providing longer polling hours may enable busy people to get to the polls.

. . . .

Answer: a. *Apathy* is defined as a lack of interest or enthusiasm. The fact that, according to the chart, more than 15% of Americans did not vote simply because they were not interested supports this opinion.

. . . .

Use the Preamble to answer the question.

Preamble to the U.S. Constitution

We the People of the United States, in Order to form a more perfect Union, establish Justice, insure domestic Tranquility, provide for the common defence, promote the general Welfare, and secure the Blessings of Liberty to ourselves and our prosperity, do ordain and establish this Constitution for the United States of America.

_____

What is the main purpose of the Preamble?
a. to tell why the Constitution is needed
b. to present an outline of the document
c. to describe the new system of government
d. to review the reasons for breaking from England

. . . .

_____

Answer: a. The Preamble lists six reasons that a new governing document is needed.

· ·

Use the cartoon to answer the following two questions.

The cartoonist would probably agree with which of the following statements?

a. The vice presidency is the second-most important position in the government.
b. Presidents should travel by elephant.
c. The vice presidency is not an important government office.
d. Everyone should dress in a top hat and a waistcoat.

Answer: c. The cartoon depicts presidential candidate Theodore Roosevelt offering the vice presidency to Joseph Cannon. The vice presidency is represented by a tiny elephant with a child's chair mounted atop. These details indicate that the cartoonist thinks the vice presidency is an insignificant job.

The cartoon shows Theodore Roosevelt, a presidential candidate in 1904, and Joseph Cannon, a man whom Roosevelt wanted for his vice president.

What is the most likely explanation for why Roosevelt is riding an elephant?

a. The elephant is a universal symbol of wealth and prosperity.
b. Roosevelt was the Republican candidate for president.
c. Roosevelt was born in India, a place where it is not unusual for people to ride elephants.
d. Roosevelt was well known as a champion of animal rights.

. . . .

Answer: b. The elephant is the symbol of the Republican Party, the party to which Theodore Roosevelt belonged. None of the other answer choices is supported by details in the cartoon.

· ·

Read the passage and answer the following two questions.

The U.S. Constitution does not explicitly give the power of judicial review to the Supreme Court. In fact, the Court did not use this power—which gives it the authority to invalidate laws and executive actions if they conflict with the Constitution—until the 1803 case of *Marbury v. Madison*. In that case, Chief Justice John Marshall ruled that a statute was unconstitutional. He argued that judicial review was necessary if the Court was to fulfill its duty of upholding the Constitution. Without it, he felt that the legislature would have a "real and practical omnipotence." Moreover, several of the Constitution's framers expected the Court to act in this way. Alexander Hamilton and James Madison emphasized the importance of judicial review in the *Federalist Papers*, a series of essays promoting the adoption of the Constitution. However, the power of judicial review continues to be a controversial power because it allows the justices—who are appointed rather than elected—to overturn laws made by Congress and state lawmaking bodies.

Which of the following statements is an implication of judicial review?
a. The Constitution is a historic document with little influence over how the government operates today.
b. The Constitution must explicitly state which branch of government is to have what authority.
c. The framers never meant for the Supreme Court to have this power.
d. The Constitution is a living document that continues to be interpreted.

. . . .

Which of the following best describes the process of judicial review?
a. to declare a law unconstitutional
b. to follow public opinion polls
c. to determine the country's changing needs
d. to propose new laws

. . . .

Answer: d. Through judicial review, the Supreme Court is continually interpreting the limits set by the Constitution.

Answer: a. According to the passage, judicial review is "the authority to invalidate laws and executive actions if they conflict with the Constitution." Choice a is a good paraphrase of the excerpt from the passage.

Read the quotation and answer the following three questions.

"Today, education is perhaps the most important function of state and local governments. Compulsory school attendance laws and the great expenditures for education both demonstrate our recognition of the importance of education to our democratic society. It is required in the performance of our most basic public responsibilities, even service in the armed forces. It is the very foundation of good citizenship. Today it is a principal instrument in awakening the child to cultural values, in preparing him for later professional training, and in helping him to adjust normally to his environment. In these days, it is doubtful that any child may reasonably be expected to succeed in life if he is denied the opportunity of an education. Such an opportunity, where the state has undertaken to provide it, is a right which must be made available to all on equal terms.

"We come then to the question presented: Does segregation of children in public schools solely on the basis of race, even though the physical facilities and other 'tangible' factors may be equal, deprive the children of the minority group of equal educational opportunities? We believe that it does."

—U.S. Supreme Court Chief Justice Earl Warren in a 1954 decision that ruled that separate schools for African Americans and whites were unconstitutional

Source: Legal Information Institute, Cornell Law School, *Brown v. Board of Education of Topeka*

Which of the following is NOT a value of education as expressed in the quotation?
a. to expose children to music and the arts
b. to explain the government's education budget
c. to prepare those who might serve the country as soldiers
d. to produce good citizens

_____

Answer: b. The amount of money the government spends on education shows that people care about education; it is not, however, a value of education as previously defined.

· ·

Sovereignty is the power or authority of a government. At one time, people believed that governments ruled by divine right, with power granted by God. Today's democratic governments receive their sovereignty from the people. By what means do the people demonstrate sovereignty in a democracy?

a. crowning a king
b. serving in the armed forces
c. voting on issues
d. obeying the law

. . . .

According to the passage, how might the Court define "equal educational opportunity"?

a. schools with the same quality of teaching
b. schools with the same quality of facilities and materials
c. schools that only admit students based on sex
d. schools that are of the same quality and welcome all students regardless of race

. . . .

Chief Justice Warren most likely mentions compulsory school attendance and government spending on education in order to

a. argue that the government should reduce its efforts in the field of education.
b. support the position that segregated schools are not inherently unequal.
c. encourage young Americans to remain in school long enough to get a high school diploma.
d. strengthen the argument that education is a critical function of government.

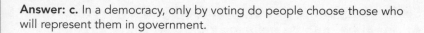

Answer: c. In a democracy, only by voting do people choose those who will represent them in government.

. . . .

Answer: d. The Court's decision states that a similar level of "physical facilities and other 'tangible' factors" is not enough to offer equal educational opportunity. You can infer that the Court believes schools should also welcome students of all races.

. . . .

Answer: d. By pointing out that the government requires students to attend school, Warren makes the point that American society places a strong emphasis on the need for a good education. Similarly, government spending on education indicates that education is a major priority in American society. Both of these facts support the argument that education is a critical function of government.

Read the passage and answer the following question.

The Sixth Amendment of the U.S.Constitution states, "In all criminal prosecutions, the accused shall enjoy the right to a speedy and public trial, by an impartial jury of the State and district wherein the crime shall have been committed, which district shall have been previously ascertained by law, and to be informed of the nature and cause of the accusation; to be confronted with the witnesses against him; to have compulsory process for obtaining witnesses in his favor, and to have the Assistance of Counsel for his defence [sic]."

_____

Which of the following instances is NOT protected by the Sixth Amendment?

a. a person accused of a crime silently prays before his trial begins

b. a person accused of drug trafficking hires a lawyer to defend him

c. a trial is moved to another area because no jurors could be found who had not heard of the crime and had an opinion about who committed it

d. a lawyer informs an accused person of her charges

. . . .

Answer: a. Prayer is protected by the First Amendment, which protects the freedom of religion.

Use the campaign poster to answer the following question.

Pro Quarterback Bill Wyoming Says:

"Vote for Sylvia Montanez for Governor. She'll do a *great* job!"

So don't forget:

Vote Montanez on Election Day!

Which of the following questions would be most useful in determining the value of the information presented on Governor Montanez's campaign sign?
a. What is Bill Wyoming's definition of "great"?
b. What qualifies Bill Wyoming to predict the quality of a future governor?
c. How good a season did Bill Wyoming have last year?
d. Does Bill Wyoming live in Sylvia Montanez's state?

. . . .

Answer: b. The campaign poster suggests that voters should choose Governor Montanez because professional quarterback Bill Wyoming thinks Montanez would be a great governor. This is typical of endorsement advertisements, which try to persuade voters by associating the candidate with a popular figure. To determine whether the information on the poster is valuable in determining whether to vote for Montanez, the voter should ask herself whether Wyoming has any expertise in the field of governing. Why should the voter care who Bill Wyoming thinks would make a great governor if Wyoming is not an expert in this area?

Isolationism refers to the national policy of avoiding political or economic relations with other countries. Which of the following is an example of American isolationist policy?

a. the Neutrality Act of 1935, an arms embargo designed to try to keep the United States out of a European war
b. bombing al-Qaeda training camps in Afghanistan after the terrorist attack on the World Trade Center
c. the unsuccessful attempt to overthrow Cuban leader Fidel Castro in 1961
d. joining with 11 nations to form the North Atlantic Treaty Organization (NATO) in 1949

. . . .

Answer: a. An example of American isolationist policy is the 1935 Neutrality Act because it was an instance of avoiding political and economic alliances with other countries.

· ·

Use the chart to answer the following question.

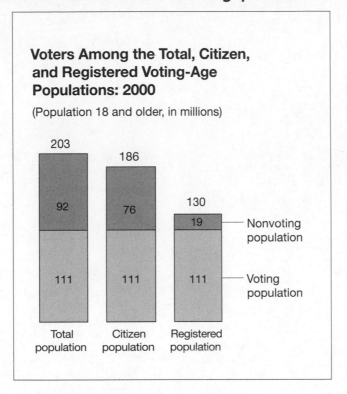

Voters Among the Total, Citizen, and Registered Voting-Age Populations: 2000

(Population 18 and older, in millions)

Source: U.S. Census Bureau, Current Population Survey, 2000.

According to the graph, how many eligible U.S. citizens are NOT registered to vote?
a. 19 million
b. 56 million
c. 76 million
d. 92 million

GED® TEST SOCIAL STUDIES FLASH REVIEW

———————

Answer: b. Subtract the registered population (130 million) from the citizen population (186 million). Fifty-six million citizens are not registered to vote.

. . . .

Use the quotations to answer the following two questions.

"We might as easily reprove the east wind, or the frost, as a political party, whose members, for the most part, could give no account of their position, but stand for the defence [sic] of those interests in which they find themselves."

—Ralph Waldo Emerson (1803–1882), American essayist

"A party of order or stability, and a party of progress or reform, are both necessary elements of a healthy state of political life."

—John Stuart Mill (1806–1873), British philosopher

_____

Which of the following party systems would Emerson most likely support?
a. **one in which citizens are loyal to a political party at all costs**
b. **a single-party system**
c. **a system with a liberal party that advocates for change and a conservative party that maintains tradition**
d. **one in which citizens are independent and think for themselves**

· ·

Which of the following party systems would Mill most likely support?
a. **one in which citizens are loyal to a political party at all costs**
b. **a single-party system**
c. **a system with a liberal party that advocates for change and a conservative party that maintains tradition**
d. **one in which citizens are independent and think for themselves**

· ·

_____

Answer: d. Emerson portrays loyal party members as followers who cannot defend the positions of their own party. Emerson would most likely choose a system that encourages individual thought.

. . . .

Answer: c. Mill believes that a healthy system needs political parties with the opposing goals of change and order.

. . . .

Use the form to answer the following two questions.

Voter Registration Application
For U.S. Citizens

You can use this form to: • register to vote • report that your name or address has changed • register with a party		This space for office use only.	

Please print in blue or black ink

1 Mr. Mrs. Miss Ms. | Last Name | First Name | Middle Name(s) | (Circle one) Jr Sr II III IV

2 Address (see instructions) – Street (or route and box number) | Apt. or Lot # | City/Town | State | Zip Code

3 Address Where You Get Your Mail If Different From Above (see instructions) | City/Town | State | Zip Code

4 Date of Birth __/__/__ Month Day Year | **5** Telephone Number (optional) | **6** ID Number (see item 6 in the instructions for your State)

7 Choice of Party (see item 7 in the instructions for your State) | **8** Race or Ethnic Group (see item 8 in the instructions for your State)

9 I swear/affirm that:
• I am a United States citizen
• I meet the eligibility requirements of my state and subscribe to any oath required.
(See item 9 in the instructions for your state before you sign.)
• The information I have provided is true to the best of my knowledge under penalty of perjury. If I have provided false information, I may be fined, imprisoned, or (if not a U.S. citizen) deported from or refused entry to the United States.

Please sign full name (or put mark) ↓

Date: __/__/__ Month Day Year

10 If the applicant is unable to sign, who helped the applicant fill out this application? Give name, address and phone number (phone number optional).

Fold here

Please fill out the sections below if they apply to you.

If this application is for a **change of name,** what was your name before you changed it?

A Mr. Mrs. Miss Ms. | Last Name | First Name | Middle Name(s) | (Circle one) Jr Sr II III IV

If you were **registered before** but this is the first time you are registering from the address in Box 2, what was your address where you were registered before?

B Street (or route and box number) | Apt. or Lot # | City/Town | State | Zip Code

If you live in a rural area but do not have a street number, or if you have no address, please show on the map where you live.

C
• Write in the names of the crossroads (or streets) nearest to where you live.
• Draw an **X** to show where you live.
• Use a dot to show any schools, churches, stores, or other landmarks near where you live, and write the name of the landmark.

NORTH ↑

Example
Route #2
• Grocery Store
Woodchuck Road
Public School ● X

To Mail:
1. Address the back of this application (see address under your state).
2. Remove plastic strip below.
3. Fold form at middle and seal at top.
4. Put on a first-class stamp and mail.

Which of the following is NOT a purpose of this form?
a. notifying the government that you have changed your name
b. registering with a political party
c. applying for U.S. citizenship
d. registering to vote in an upcoming local election

Answer: c. You cannot use this form to apply for U.S. citizenship. The uses of the form appear in its upper left-hand corner.

Which of the following expresses a FACT rather than an opinion?

a. States have different requirements about who is eligible to vote.
b. The voting age should be changed from 18 to 21 years of age.
c. Every state should institute a "voter-motor" program in which people can register to vote at the same time that they are registering their motor vehicle.
d. The government should allow non-citizens to vote.

. . . .

Answer: a. The information on the voter registration form provides proof that choice a is a statement of fact.

Use the following definitions of political beliefs and policies to answer the following four questions.

Isolationism: a national policy of avoiding political alliances with other nations
Nationalism: a sense of allegiance to the interests and culture of a nation
Socialism: the belief that essential property and services should be owned and managed by the government
Pacifism: the belief that nations should settle their disputes peacefully
Regionalism: a political division between two regions within an area

Read the quotation and identify which term best describes it.

"This whole nation of one hundred and thirty million free men, women, and children is becoming one great fighting force. Some of us are soldiers or sailors, some of us are civilians. . . . A few of us are decorated with medals for heroic achievement, but all of us can have that deep and permanent inner satisfaction that comes from doing the best we know how—each of us playing an honorable part in the great struggle to save our democratic civilization."

—Radio address of Franklin D. Roosevelt, October 12, 1942

a. **isolationism**
b. **nationalism**
c. **socialism**
d. **pacifism**

Answer: b. The purpose of Roosevelt's address was to inspire a spirit of nationalism during World War II.

· ·

Use the chart to answer the following two questions.

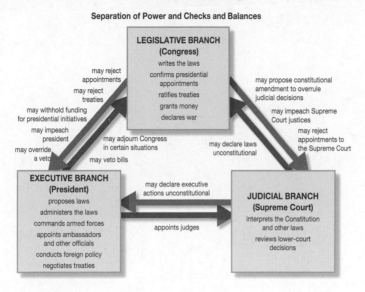

Separation of Power and Checks and Balances

The most important way that the Supreme Court can check the power of Congress is to
a. veto bills.
b. shorten legislative terms.
c. declare laws unconstitutional.
d. initiate impeachment proceedings.

. . . .

——————————

Answer: c. The power to declare a law unconstitutional is an important check of the Supreme Court on the legislature.

· ·

How do the president and Congress share wartime power?

a. Only Congress can declare war, but the president commands the armed forces.

b. The president can declare war, but Congress must authorize funds for the military.

c. Congress and the president work together to command the armed forces and negotiate peace treaties.

d. Congress declares war, but only the president can write laws after a war is declared.

· ·

Answer: a. Only Congress has power to declare war, and the president serves as commander in chief over the military.

. . . .

Use the cartoon to answer the following question.

November 11, 1871

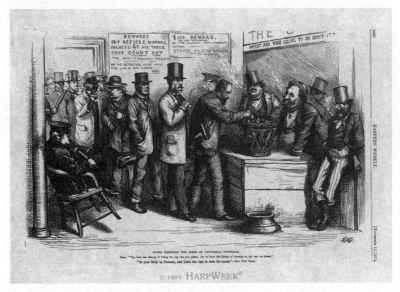

Political Boss: "You have the liberty of Voting for any one you please; but we have the Liberty of Counting in any one we please."

_____

What is the main point of the political cartoon above, "Going Through the Form of Universal Suffrage?"

a. Voting is a privilege to be earned by the citizenry.
b. Voters should always cast their ballots strictly along party lines.
c. Universal suffrage is meaningless when political bosses control the ballot box.
d. Voting is the right of every working person.

———————

Answer: c. The cartoon, with its caption, shows men voting while a political boss and his cronies watch. The boss's comment makes it clear that voting is an empty exercise when a boss will declare his candidate elected, no matter what the vote count. This choice reflects the point of the cartoon.

· ·

Read the quotation and identify which term best describes it.

"The . . . parties solemnly declare in the names of their respective peoples that they condemn recourse to war for the solution of international controversies, and renounce it as an instrument of national policy in their relations with one another."

—Kellogg-Briand Pact, Article I, 1928

a. **isolationism**
b. **nationalism**
c. **socialism**
d. **pacifism**

. . . .

Read the quotation and identify which term best describes it.

"The great rule of conduct for us in regard to foreign nations is, in extending our commercial relations, to have with them as little political connection as possible. So far as we have already formed engagements let them be fulfilled with perfect good faith."

—President George Washington, Farewell Address, 1796

a. **isolationism**
b. **consumerism**
c. **socialism**
d. **pacifism**

. . . .

Answer: d. Signed by the United States and 15 other nations, the *Kellogg-Briand Pact of 1928* tried to promote pacifism. However, because there was no way to enforce the pact, it was not effective.

• •

Answer: a. Washington advocates avoiding political attachments with other nations, which is an isolationist view.

• •

Read the quotation and identify which term best describes it.

"The free States alone, if we must go on alone, will make a glorious nation. Twenty millions in the temperate zone, stretching from the Atlantic to the Pacific, full of vigor, industry, inventive genius, educated, and moral; increasing by immigration rapidly, and, above all, free—all free—will form a confederacy of twenty States scarcely inferior in real power to the unfortunate Union of thirty-three States which we had on the first of November."

—Rutherford Birchard Hayes, January 4, 1861

a. **isolationism**
b. **nationalism**
c. **socialism**
d. **regionalism**

GED® TEST SOCIAL STUDIES FLASH REVIEW

Answer: d. This comment demonstrates the political division between the North and South before the outbreak of the Civil War.

· ·

Review the map and answer the following three questions.

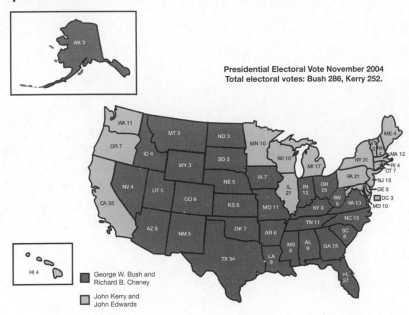

Presidential Electoral Vote November 2004
Total electoral votes: Bush 286, Kerry 252.

■ George W. Bush and Richard B. Cheney

□ John Kerry and John Edwards

The electoral college is a group of electors who choose the president and vice president. Each state is allowed the same number of electors as its total number of U.S. senators and representatives—so each state has at least three electors. In most states, the candidate who wins the most popular votes earns that state's electoral votes.

Source: National Archives and Records Administration.

Based on the information in the map, which of the following might be true of Kerry's campaign strategy?

a. It focused on winning the states in the Southeast.
b. Kerry targeted his campaign efforts in his home state of Massachusetts.
c. It targeted states that have large populations and a large number of electoral votes.
d. It focused on winning most of the states with small populations.

_____

Answer: c. You can infer from the map that Kerry's campaign strategy focused on winning states with large populations and a large number of electoral votes, like California, Illinois, New York, Pennsylvania, and Michigan.

Which of the following is NOT a true statement?
a. George W. Bush won a larger number of states.
b. John Kerry was popular in New England.
c. If Kerry had won Florida's electoral votes, he would have become president.
d. If Kerry had won South Dakota's electoral votes, he would have become president.

. . . .

Which of the following conclusions can you make from the information in the map?
a. Women are more likely than men to vote for the Democratic party.
b. Increasing numbers of Americans consider themselves political independents.
c. The Sunbelt—the southern and southwestern states— was once a stronghold of the democratic party.
d. There were distinct regional differences in voting patterns.

. . . .

Answer: d. Had Kerry won South Dakota's three electoral votes, the final electoral vote total would have been Bush 283, Kerry 255. Therefore, Kerry's winning in South Dakota would not have been enough to change the results of the election. In contrast, had Kerry won in Florida (choice c), the final electoral vote would have been Kerry 279, Bush 259 (you must remember to add Florida's 27 votes to Kerry's total AND subtract Florida's 27 votes from Bush's total).

• •

Answer: d. The map highlights the regional differences in the 2004 presidential election. Bush was clearly more popular in the southern and mountain states; Kerry was clearly more popular in the Northeast and on the Pacific coast. The map does not provide any information to support any of the other statements.

• •

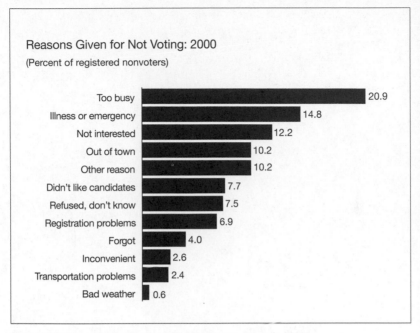

Reasons Given for Not Voting: 2000
(Percent of registered nonvoters)

Reason	Percent
Too busy	20.9
Illness or emergency	14.8
Not interested	12.2
Out of town	10.2
Other reason	10.2
Didn't like candidates	7.7
Refused, don't know	7.5
Registration problems	6.9
Forgot	4.0
Inconvenient	2.6
Transportation problems	2.4
Bad weather	0.6

Source: U.S. Census Bureau, Current Population Survey, November 2000.

Based on the information in the graph, which of the following proposals might best improve the voting rate?
a. **Distribute umbrellas to all households to encourage people to vote on rainy election days.**
b. **Organize buses to help people get to voting places.**
c. **Send reminders to registered voters so they do not forget to vote.**
d. **Reschedule Election Day to a weekend so that people who are busy at work and at school can be available to vote.**

. . . .

_____

Answer: d. Because the most common reason for not voting is "too busy," it is reasonable to conclude that rescheduling Election Day to a day when many people are not at work may improve the voting rate.

. . . .

Read the passage and answer the following two questions.

The U.S. Constitution gives the president the power to veto, or reject, a bill passed by Congress. The president typically states his objections to the bill when he announces the veto. Because it takes a two-thirds vote from both the House of Representatives and the Senate to override a veto, Congress often changes the bill to make it more acceptable to the president. Sometimes Congress adds provisions to a bill that the president strongly favors. The president does not have the power of line-item veto, in which lines or parts of a bill can be rejected individually. The president must accept or reject the bill as Congress has written it.

_____

Which of the following statements can you infer from the passage?
a. **Congress is more powerful than the president.**
b. **Congress tries to get the president to accept its provisions by attaching provisions to a bill that the president supports.**
c. **A president is more effective when members of the same political party are the majority in Congress.**
d. **If a president vetoes a bill, there is no way to get it passed into law.**

. . . .

Which of the following conclusions can you make based on the passage?
a. **It is easier to rewrite and make a bill more acceptable to the president than it is to override a veto.**
b. **It is easier to override a veto than it is to rewrite and make a bill more acceptable to the president.**
c. **The U.S. Constitution gives the president the power to edit the bills he receives from Congress.**
d. **The system of checks and balances insures that the president has no influence over the lawmaking branch of government.**

. . . .

—————————

Answer: b. Because the president cannot reject single items within a bill, he must accept them if he wants the provisions he favors to become law.

· ·

Answer: a. Because Congress would rather rewrite a bill than try to override a veto, you can conclude that it is easier to do so.

· ·

Read the passage below and answer the following four questions.

California Voter Guide

California Legislative Races

The California State Legislature is made up of two houses: the senate and the assembly. The senate is the upper house. There are 40 senators, each representing about 800,000 people. The assembly is the lower house. There are 80 assembly members, each representing about 400,000 people. Senators and assembly members receive an annual salary of $99,000 plus per diem; legislative leaders receive a slightly higher salary.

Assembly members are elected to two-year terms and are limited to serving three terms. Senators are elected to four-year terms and are limited to serving two terms. California's legislative districts are "nested," so that two assembly districts comprise one senate district.

The California Voter Foundation has compiled information on each of this year's 80 state assembly races and 20 state senate races. (Half the senate seats are up for election in each election year—this year the odd-numbered seats are up.) In this guide you will find a list of the candidates running in each district, their party affiliation, and contact information. You will also learn how to access candidates' websites, which typically feature campaign literature, endorsement lists, position papers, and information about how to contribute or volunteer.

———————————

Based on the guide, which statement is true about California legislators?

a. **Each senator represents more people than each assembly member.**

b. **Each assembly member represents more people than each senator.**

c. **Senators have term limits, but assembly members do not.**

d. **Assembly members have term limits, but senators do not.**

. . . .

Answer: a. Each senator represents 800,000 people, but each assembly member represents 400,000.

. . . .

Why won't voters choose all of California's state senators in the next election?
a. Some senate seats have term limits.
b. Typically only half of eligible voters vote.
c. California's legislative districts are "nested."
d. Only half the senate seats are up for election in any election year.

. . . .

If a California assembly member was first elected in 2008, in 2012 the assembly member
a. was not allowed to run again.
b. could run for two more terms.
c. could run for one more term.
d. was not allowed to run that year but could run in 2013.

. . . .

Based on the Guide, if you live in an odd-numbered district, you
a. can only vote for senator in the coming election.
b. may vote for both assembly member and senator in the coming election.
c. are represented only by a senator.
d. are represented only by an assembly member.

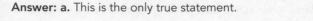

Answer: a. This is the only true statement.

. . . .

Answer: c. Assembly members are elected to two-year terms and may serve for three terms. So an assembly member would have served two terms from 1996 to 2000. Therefore, he or she could serve one more term.

. . . .

Answer: b. Odd-numbered senate seats are up for election this year, so you would vote for a senator and an assembly member, since there is an election for assembly members every two years.

GED® TEST SOCIAL STUDIES FLASH REVIEW

Sovereignty is the power or authority of a government. At one time, people believed that governments ruled by divine right, with power granted by God. Today's democratic governments receive their sovereignty from the people. By what means do the people demonstrate sovereignty in a democracy?

a. crowning a king
b. serving in the armed forces
c. voting on issues
d. attending religious services

Answer: c. In a democracy, only by voting do people choose who will represent them in government.

· ·

Which conclusion can most fairly be drawn from the two excerpts?

Excerpt from the Majority Decision of
Plessy v. Ferguson (1896)

This case turns upon the constitutionality of an act of the general assembly of the state of Louisiana, passed in 1890, providing for separate railway carriages for the white and colored races. . . . The constitutionality of this act is attacked upon the ground that it conflicts . . . with . . . the Fourteenth Amendment, which prohibits certain restrictive legislation on the part of the states.

The object of the [Fourteenth] Amendment was undoubtedly to enforce the absolute equality of the two races before the law, but . . . it could not have been intended to abolish distinctions based upon color . . . Legislation is powerless to eradicate racial instincts or to abolish distinctions based upon physical differences.

Excerpt from the Majority Decision of
Brown v. Board of Education (1954)

To separate [children in grade and high schools] from others of similar age and qualifications solely because of their race generates a feeling of inferiority as to their status in the community that may affect their hearts and minds in a way unlikely to ever be undone. . . . Whatever may have been the extent of psychological knowledge at the time of *Plessy v. Ferguson*, this finding is amply supported by modern authority . . .

We conclude that in the field of public education the doctrine of "separate but equal" has no place. Separate educational facilities are inherently unequal. Therefore, we hold that the plaintiffs and other similarly situated . . . are . . . deprived of the equal protection of the laws guaranteed by the Fourteenth Amendment.

—Justice Henry Brown

a. **The U.S. Supreme Court occasionally changes its mind.**
b. **It is impossible to make laws to eliminate racial instincts.**
c. **Interpretive problems can be solved by returning to the actual words of the Constitution.**
d. **Checks and balances has no effect on the federal system.**

. . . .

Answer: a. *Brown* did overturn *Plessy*.

Use the chart below to answer the following question.

Residency Requirements for Voting

State	Residency Requirement
California	Must be a registered voter 29 days before an election; 20-day residency requirement
Colorado	25-day residency requirement
Illinois	30-day residency requirement
Kansas	14-day residency requirement
Missouri	No durational residency requirement; must be registered by the fourth Wednesday prior to election

---

An election is to be held on Tuesday, November 6. In which of these states would someone who moved to the state on Monday, October 1, and registered immediately be allowed to vote?
a. California only
b. California and Kansas only
c. all the states listed except Missouri
d. all the states listed

. . . .

Answer: d. None of the states in the chart has a residency requirement of more than 30 days. The time from October 1 to November 6 is more than 30 days. If someone registered immediately, the registration requirements of California and Missouri would have been met. Thus, choice d is the best answer.

Use this excerpt from the Declaration of Independence to answer the following two questions.

IN CONGRESS, July 4, 1776.

The unanimous Declaration of the thirteen united States of America,

When in the Course of human events, it becomes necessary for one people to dissolve the political bands which have connected them with another . . . a decent respect to the opinions of mankind requires that they should declare the causes which impel them to the separation.

We hold these truths to be self-evident, that all men are created equal, that they are endowed by their Creator with certain unalienable Rights, that among these are Life, Liberty and the pursuit of Happiness. . . . That whenever any Form of Government becomes destructive of these ends, it is the Right of the People to alter or to abolish it, and to institute new Government. . . . Prudence, indeed, will dictate that Governments long established should not be changed for light and transient causes; and accordingly all experience hath shewn, that mankind are more disposed to suffer, while evils are sufferable, than to right themselves by abolishing the forms to which they are accustomed. But when a long train of abuses and usurpations, pursuing invariably the same Object evinces a design to reduce them under absolute Despotism, it is their right, it is their duty, to throw off such Government, and to provide new Guards for their future security. . . .

_____

Which best states the meaning of *unalienable* in the excerpt?
a. absolute
b. historical
c. resolute
d. governmental

. . . .

_____

Answer: a. Unalienable rights are explained in the excerpt. Based on the explanation, they are absolute rights to which people are entitled.

· ·

Based on the excerpt, which type of government are people generally least likely to move forward to "throw off"?
a. an oppressive government that is new to the people
b. a government that has been governing unfairly for a long time
c. an undemocratic government with self-serving motives
d. a recently formed government that commits multiple offenses against the people

. . . .

Accessed through Northwestern University Library:
https://images.northwestern.edu/multiresimages/
inu:dil-a77d6c09-ad92-4ffa-a762-ce918cdaca2e

_____

Based on the details in the poster, what is referenced by the shadow in the image?
a. Russian communism
b. Fascism in Italy
c. Japanese imperialism
d. Nazi Germany

. . . .

Answer: b. The excerpt states: "mankind are more disposed to suffer, while evils are sufferable, than to right themselves by abolishing the forms to which they are accustomed," so people are likely to be accustomed to an unfair government that has been governing for a long time, and they are less likely to move forward to "throw off" this type of government.

Answer: d. The shadow in the image forms the shape of a swastika, the symbol of Nazi Germany.

Use the statement below, made by Sir Winston Churchill, to answer the following question.

"Democracy is the worst form of government, except for all those other forms that have been tried from time to time."

—Speech to House of Commons
November 11, 1947

_____

Based on the quote, it is clear Churchill believed that
a. democracy was the worst form of government that had been practiced by commoners.
b. improvements could be made to democracy, but it was the best form of government to date.
c. democracy was an extremely flawed form of government that should not be abandoned.
d. changes to democracy should not be implemented, but other known forms of government should be implemented instead.

. . . .

———————

Answer: b. Churchill stated that democracy was the worst form of government except for earlier forms of government that had been tried.

· ·

Use the information below to answer the following question.

Requirements to Serve as U.S. President

✔ must be at least 35 years old
✔ must be a U.S. resident for at least 14 years
✔ must be a native-born U.S. citizen (or have been born in a country other than the United States to a parent who was a U.S. citizen at the time)

Based *ONLY* on the information above, it is clear that which of the following would not meet the requirements to serve as U.S. president?

a. a person who was born in the United States, is 41 years old, and has lived in the United States for 41 years
b. a person who is 68 years old, was born in France to a mother who was a U.S. citizen, and has lived in the United States for 51 years
c. a person who was born in the United States, is 34 years old, and has lived in the United States for 34 years
d. a person who is 50 years old and was a U.S. resident for 10 years, left the United States for 36 years, and then returned to live in the United States for 4 years

· ·

Answer: c. This person is 34, and the requirements state that a person must be at least 35 in order to serve as U.S. president.

· ·

Use the following passage to answer the question.

Article I, Section 3 of the United States Constitution

The Senate of the United States shall be composed of two Senators from each state, chosen by the legislature thereof for six years; and each Senator shall have one Vote.

_____

Which statement regarding election of U.S. senators is not accurate?

a. Today, senators may serve nationally, even if they lack local legislative service.

b. Senators are chosen today in the same way as they were chosen during the 1700s.

c. Today, each state has two senators, just as there have been since the earliest senatorial elections.

d. Senators are elected to pass legislation today, just as they were chosen to pass legislation during the 1700s.

. . . .

_____

Answer: b. The title provides the detail that this article is part of the U.S. Constitution; it is not an amendment to the U.S. Constitution. This means it became the law of the land in 1776. The article provides for state legislatures to select senators, and this is not the method of selection for senators today. Today, voters choose senators.

Use the paragraph and map below to answer the following two questions.

In 1949, fear arose due to the pressure of a potential attack by the Soviet Union after World War II. A number of countries came together with an interest in developing military security. They formed the North Atlantic Treaty Organization (NATO). Each nation belonging to NATO made a promise to defend other members against an attack from a non-member nation. Due to events that arose shortly after the formation of NATO, the Soviet Union created alliances with other communist countries in a pact that came to be known as the Warsaw Pact.

NATO still exists today. It works to address many difficult and complex international issues.

NATO Members (2014)

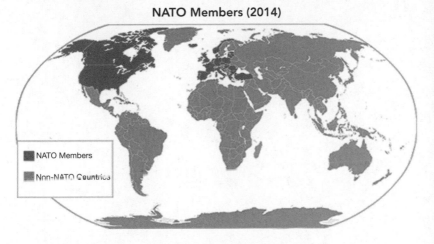

NATO Members

Non-NATO Countries

Which question can be answered, based solely on information in the paragraph and the map?
a. **Was Russia a member of NATO in 2014?**
b. **During which year was the Warsaw Pact signed?**
c. **Which countries were the initial members of NATO in 1949?**
d. **How many issues were addressed by the Warsaw Pact?**

Answer: a. The map, key, and date in the map title make it clear that Russia was not a member of NATO in 2014.

Use the quote below to answer the following question.

Of the various forms of government which have prevailed in the world, an hereditary monarchy seems to present the fairest scope for ridicule. Is it possible to relate without an indignant smile, that, on the father's decease, the property of a nation, like that of a drove of oxen, descends to his infant son, as yet unknown to mankind and to himself, and that the bravest warriors and the wisest statesmen, relinquishing their natural right to empire, approach the royal cradle with bended knees and protestations of inviolable fidelity?

—from *The History of the Decline and Fall of the Roman Empire, Volume 1*
by Edward Gibbon, Esq.
Published in London in 1862

_____

Which phrase from the excerpt provides the clearest example of the author's viewpoint regarding a monarchy?
a. **various forms of government**
b. **prevailed in the world**
c. **the property of a nation**
d. **like a drove of oxen**

Answer: d. The author is comparing the passage of property for a nation to the passing down of livestock within a family. This clearly shows the author's point of view.

· ·

Fill in the blank with the correct term.

The _____ is a layer of gases above the planet's surface.
a. biosphere
b. lithosphere
c. topography
d. atmosphere

. . . .

Fill in the blank with the correct term.

_____ is/are opposite in the Northern and Southern Hemispheres.
a. The tilt of Earth
b. Earth's orbit
c. The seasons of the year
d. Earth's axis

. . . .

Fill in the blank with the correct term.

_____ include(s) the atmosphere, oceans, freshwater systems, geological formations, and soils of Earth.
a. Habitat
b. The biosphere
c. Biodiversity
d. Mineral resources

Answer: d. The atmosphere is a layer of gases above the planet's surface.

· ·

Answer: c. The seasons of the year are opposite in the Northern and Southern Hemispheres.

· ·

Answer: b. The biosphere includes the atmosphere, oceans, freshwater systems, geological formations, and soils of Earth.

Fill in the blank with the correct term.

_____ geography deals with Earth's physical features like climate, land, air, water, plants, and animal life and their relationship to each other and humans.

a. Physical
b. Cultural
c. Human
d. Political

. . . .

Fill in the blank with the correct term.

_____ is the study of population.

a. Hydrology
b. Demography
c. Climatology
d. Technology

. . . .

Fill in the blank with the correct term.

Oceans, rivers, lakes, and other bodies of water make up the water-based _____.

a. water cycle
b. evaporation
c. hydrosphere
d. run-off

Answer: a. Physical geography deals with Earth's physical features like climate, land, air, water, plants, and animal life and their relationship to each other and humans.

. . . .

Answer: b. Demography is the study of population.

. . . .

Answer: c. Oceans, rivers, lakes, and other bodies of water make up the water-based hydrosphere.

Fill in the blank with the correct term.

International planners use the term _____ to describe where freshwater needs are greatest.
a. precipitation
b. water stress
c. urban sewage
d. condensation

. . . .

Fill in the blank with the correct term.

The _____ is surface land including the continents and ocean floors.
a. lithosphere
b. atmosphere
c. biosphere
d. hydrosphere

. . . .

Fill in the blank with the correct term.

Plate _____ created Earth's largest features, like continents, oceans, and mountain ranges.
a. pollution
b. irrigation
c. flooding
d. tectonics

Answer: b. International planners use the term *water stress* to describe where freshwater needs are greatest.

· ·

Answer: a. The lithosphere is surface land, including the continents and ocean floors.

· ·

Answer: d. Plate tectonics created Earth's largest features, like continents, oceans, and mountain ranges.

Fill in the blank with the correct term.

Water _____ wear(s) away soil and rock.
a. desalination
b. erosion
c. valleys
d. cycles

· ·

Fill in the blank with the correct term.

_____ protect(s) soil from wind erosion.
a. Urbanization
b. Deserts
c. Glaciers
d. Plants

· ·

Fill in the blank with the correct term.

_____, including aerial photography and satellite imaging, is used to know more about mineral deposits and freshwater sources, as well as to survey human activities.
a. Cartography
b. Remote sensing
c. Direct observation
d. A key

Answer: b. Water erosion wears away soil and rock.

. . . .

Answer: d. Plants protect soil from wind erosion.

. . . .

Answer: b. Remote sensing, including aerial photography and satellite imaging, is used to know more about mineral deposits and freshwater sources, as well as to survey human activities.

Fill in the blank with the correct term.

The _____ is 0° latitude.
a. equator
b. prime meridian
c. North Pole
d. absolute location

. . . .

Fill in the blank with the correct term.

Most ancient civilizations began in _____.
a. mountains
b. river valleys
c. deserts
d. plateaus

. . . .

Fill in the blank with the correct term.

The raising and grazing of livestock, or _____, is a
way of life for people living on the steppes.
a. agriculture
b. aquaculture
c. pastoralism
d. terracing

Answer: a. The equator is 0° latitude.

. . . .

Answer: b. Most ancient civilizations began in river valleys.

. . . .

Answer: c. The raising and grazing of livestock, or pastoralism, is a way of life for people living on the steppes.

Fill in the blank with the correct term.

Arab expansion brought _____ to North Africa, Southwest Asia, and Central Asia.
a. Hinduism
b. Buddhism
c. Judaism
d. Islam

. . . .

Fill in the blank with the correct term.

In the 1980s, the U.S. Central Intelligence Agency (CIA) financed Osama bin Laden's fight against the Russians in the mountains of _____.
a. Iraq
b. Afghanistan
c. Iran
d. Pakistan

. . . .

Fill in the blank with the correct term.

_____ is a means of managing natural resources in ways that do not deplete them or cause more damage to ecosystems.
a. Sustainable development
b. The Green Revolution
c. Outsourcing
d. Qaqortoq

Answer: d. Arab expansion brought Islam to North Africa, Southwest Asia, and Central Asia.

· ·

Answer: b. In the 1980s, the U.S. Central Intelligence Agency (CIA) financed Osama bin Laden's fight against the Russians in the mountains of Afghanistan.

· ·

Answer: a. Sustainable development is a means of managing natural resources in ways that do not deplete them or cause more damage to ecosystems.

Fill in the blank with the correct term.

The _____, or Continental Divide, determine(s) the flow of rivers in North America.
a. Canadian Shield
b. Great Basin
c. Appalachian Mountains
d. Rockies

· ·

Fill in the blank with the correct term.

The plains of the pampas are used for _____.
a. growing cereal grains
b. cattle ranching
c. growing ornamental plants
d. training cowboys

· ·

Fill in the blank with the correct term.

_____ is the primary language of Latin America.
a. Latin
b. English
c. French
d. Spanish

GED® TEST SOCIAL STUDIES FLASH REVIEW

Answer: d. The Rockies, or Continental Divide, determine(s) the flow of rivers in North America.

. . . .

Answer: c. The plains of the pampas are used for growing ornamental plants.

. . . .

Answer: d. Spanish is the primary language of Latin America.

Fill in the blank with the correct term.

Giant agricultural estates from the colonial era now disappearing in Latin America are called _____.
a. maquiladoras
b. caudillos
c. latifundia
d. campesinos

· ·

Fill in the blank with the correct term.

Most people in Russia live _____.
a. west of the Ural Mountains
b. in Siberia
c. in the Caucasus region
d. in the Caspian Sea republics

· ·

Fill in the blank with the correct term.

Since 1991, the Commonwealth of Independent States (CIS) has expanded its _____ economy.
a. command
b. market
c. collectivized agriculture
d. environmental degradation and

Answer: c. Giant agricultural estates from the colonial era now disappearing in Latin America are called latifundia.

. . . .

Answer: a. Most people in Russia live west of the Ural Mountains.

. . . .

Answer: b. Since 1991, the Commonwealth of Independent States (CIS) has expanded its market economy.

Fill in the blank with the correct term.

Western European industry developed out of the mineral and soil resources of the _____.
a. Emerald Isle
b. Polders
c. North European Plain
d. Alps

. . . .

Fill in the blank with the correct term.

Natural vegetation of _____ latitudes includes deciduous and coniferous trees.
a. very high
b. middle
c. very low
d. all

. . . .

Fill in the blank with the correct term.

The Romance languages of French, Italian, Spanish, and Portuguese are Indo-European languages derived from _____.
a. Basque
b. Bantu
c. Latin
d. German

Answer: c. Western European industry developed out of the mineral and soil resources of the North European Plain.

. . . .

Answer: b. Natural vegetation of middle latitudes includes deciduous and coniferous trees.

. . . .

Answer: c. The Romance languages of French, Italian, Spanish, and Portuguese are Indo-European languages derived from Latin.

Fill in the blank with the correct term.

Overfarming, removing too much vegetation, and overgrazing livestock has led to _____ in Europe.
a. soil erosion
b. deforestation
c. increased vegetation, including trees,
d. soil erosion and deforestation

. . . .

Fill in the blank with the correct term.

Fossil fuel automobile exhaust causes _____.
a. acid rain, property damage, and environmental destruction
b. biofuel
c. natural gas
d. El Niño

. . . .

Fill in the blank with the correct term.

A _____ is a triangular section of land formed by sand and silt carried downriver.
a. delta
b. cataract
c. harmattan
d. tornado

Answer: d. Overfarming, removing too much vegetation, and overgrazing livestock has led to soil erosion and deforestation in Europe.

. . . .

Answer: a. Fossil fuel automobile exhaust causes acid rain, property damage, and environmental destruction.

. . . .

Answer: a. A delta is a triangular section of land formed by sand and silt carried downriver.

Fill in the blank with the correct term.

In Africa, _____ climate zones can be found near the equator.

a. tropical
b. highland
c. steppe
d. altiplano

. . . .

Fill in the blank with the correct term.

Darfur, site of a modern refugee crisis, is located in

_____.

a. Congo
b. Rwanda
c. Sudan
d. Cambodia

. . . .

Fill in the blank with the correct term.

In the colonial era, Europeans built _____ in Africa, Asia, and Latin America to acquire wealth from natural resources.

a. commercial plantations
b. railroads
c. port facilities
d. commercial plantations, railroads, and port facilities

Answer: a. In Africa, tropical climate zones can be found near the equator.

. . . .

Answer: c. Darfur, site of a modern refugee crisis, is located in Sudan.

. . . .

Answer: d. In the colonial era, Europeans built commercial plantations, railroads, and port facilities in Africa, Asia, and Latin America to acquire wealth from natural resources.

Fill in the blank with the correct term.

Tanzania's Serengeti National Park, Kenya's Masai Mara, and Ghana's Kakum National Park are all _____.
a. game reserves
b. poaching parks
c. game reserves and poaching parks
d. altiplanos

· ·

Fill in the blank with the correct term.

An undersea _____ generates a tsunami, a giant wave that gets higher as it reaches the coast.
a. tornado
b. earthquake
c. typhoon
d. archipelago

· ·

Fill in the blank with the correct term.

Most of the tens of thousands of rivers in _____ start in Tibet and empty into the Pacific Ocean.
a. China
b. Nepal
c. Japan
d. the Philippines

Answer: a. Tanzania's Serengeti National Park, Kenya's Masai Mara, and Ghana's Kakum National Park are all game reserves.

. . . .

Answer: b. An undersea earthquake generates a tsunami, a giant wave that gets higher as it reaches the coast.

. . . .

Answer: a. Most of the tens of thousands of rivers in China start in Tibet and empty into the Pacific Ocean.

Fill in the blank with the correct term.

A hurricane in the Atlantic Ocean is a(n) _____ in the Pacific Ocean.
a. avalanche
b. tsunami
c. typhoon
d. shogun

. . . .

Fill in the blank with the correct term.

The Dalai Lama is _____ Buddhist spiritual leader.
a. Nepal's
b. Japan's
c. China's
d. Tibet's

. . . .

Fill in the blank with the correct term.

Due to _____ control over natural resources in the Pacific, Japan attempted in the first half of the twentieth century to take military control of the region.
a. Western
b. Chinese
c. Arab
d. East Indian

Answer: c. A hurricane in the Atlantic Ocean is a typhoon in the Pacific Ocean.

. . . .

Answer: d. The Dalai Lama is Tibet's Buddhist spiritual leader.

. . . .

Answer: a. Due to Western control over natural resources in the Pacific, Japan attempted in the first half of the twentieth century to take military control of the region.

Fill in the blank with the correct term.

Chinese and Korean governments have been most influenced by _____.

a. Taoism
b. Buddhism
c. Confucianism
d. Shintoism

. . . .

Which of the following is true about China?

a. It is heavily polluting the environment by rapidly burning fossil fuels.
b. It is disposing of large amounts of cancerous industrial waste.
c. It is a member of the World Trade Organization (WTO).
d. All of the above.

. . . .

Fill in the blank with the correct term.

The Philippines, Indonesia, and Malaysia are all _____.

a. landlocked in Southeast Asia
b. part of mainland Southeast Asia
c. archipelagoes in Southeast Asia
d. controlled by China

Answer: c. Chinese and Korean governments have been most influenced by Confucianism.

. . . .

Answer: d. All of the above.

. . . .

Answer: c. The Philippines, Indonesia, and Malaysia are all archipelagoes in Southeast Asia.

Fill in the blank with the correct term.

The _____ can only be found in Southeast Asia.
a. rhinoceros
b. minke whale
c. silkworm
d. Komodo dragon

. . . .

Fill in the blank with the correct term.

The _____ first settled in Cambodia and Vietnam.
a. Mons
b. Burmans
c. Khmers
d. Thais

. . . .

Fill in the blank with the correct term.

The _____ is a Chinese form of architecture also
found in Southeast Asia.
a. wat
b. pagoda
c. kabuki
d. kami

Answer: d. The Komodo dragon can only be found in Southeast Asia.

. . . .

Answer: c. The Khmers first settled in Cambodia and Vietnam.

. . . .

Answer: b. The pagoda is a Chinese form of architecture also found in Southeast Asia.

Fill in the blank with the correct term.

_____ is the largest Muslim country in the world and a site of terrorist attacks.
a. Iraq
b. Afghanistan
c. The Philippines
d. Indonesia

. . . .

Fill in the blank with the correct term.

On December 26, 2004, an earthquake in the Indian Ocean created a _____ that left 225,000 people dead and millions homeless.
a. typhoon
b. tsunami
c. hurricane
d. tornado

. . . .

Fill in the blank with the correct term.

_____ is the only nation in the world that is a country and continent.
a. Antarctica
b. New Zealand
c. Iceland
d. Australia

Answer: d. Indonesia is the largest Muslim country in the world and a site of terrorist attacks.

. . . .

Answer: b. On December 26, 2004, an earthquake in the Indian Ocean created a tsunami that left 225,000 people dead and millions homeless.

. . . .

Answer: d. Australia is the only nation in the world that is a country and continent.

Fill in the blank with the correct term.

The lowest temperature ever recorded occurred in

_____.

a. China
b. Russia
c. Greenland
d. United States

· ·

Which of the following is rich in mineral resources and grasslands for livestock grazing?

a. Australia
b. New Zealand
c. Antarctica
d. Australia, Antarctica, and New Zealand

· ·

Fill in the blank with the correct term.

The Earth's atmosphere is made of mostly _____.

a. oxygen
b. carbon dioxide
c. nitrogen
d. helium

Answer: b. The lowest temperature ever recorded occurred in Russia. It was observed at −128.6°F at Vostok.

· ·

Answer: a. Australia

· ·

Answer: c. The Earth's atmosphere is made of mostly nitrogen.

Fill in the blank with the correct term.

The Tropic of _____, at 23.5° N, is the northernmost point to receive direct sunlight.
a. Cancer
b. Capricorn
c. Equinox
d. Solstice

. . . .

Fill in the blank with the correct term.

A(n) _____ is a community of plants and animals dependent on one another and their surroundings to survive.
a. biosphere
b. resource
c. ecosystem
d. physical geographic process

. . . .

Fill in the blank with the correct term.

_____ geography focuses on history, government, population growth, urban development, economic production and consumption, the arts, healthcare, and education.
a. Physical
b. Habitat
c. Human or cultural
d. Transitional

Answer: a. The Tropic of Cancer, at 23.5° N, is the northernmost point to receive direct sunlight.

. . . .

Answer: c. An ecosystem is a community of plants and animals dependent on one another and their surroundings to survive.

. . . .

Answer: c. Human or cultural geography focuses on history, government, population growth, urban development, economic production and consumption, the arts, healthcare, and education.

Fill in the blank with the correct term.

Birth rates are high in the _____ world.
a. developed
b. industrial
c. Western
d. developing

· ·

Fill in the blank with the correct term.

Seas, gulfs, and bays are small _____ water bodies.
a. fresh
b. salt
c. lake
d. tributary

· ·

Fill in the blank with the correct term.

Nearly all Earth's surface water is _____ water.
a. ground
b. fresh
c. salt
d. river

Answer: d. Birth rates are high in the developing world.

. . . .

Answer: b. Seas, gulfs, and bays are small saltwater bodies.

. . . .

Answer: c. Nearly all Earth's surface water is salt water.

Fill in the blank with the correct term.

The lithosphere is Earth's _____.
a. landforms
b. mantle
c. crust
d. core

. . . .

Fill in the blank with the correct term.

The _____ of Fire is an area of earthquake and volcanic activity that crosses continents and oceans.
a. Magma
b. Trench
c. Slope
d. Ring

. . . .

Fill in the blank with the correct term.

As glaciers melt and recede, they leave large piles of rock and debris known as _____.
a. icebergs
b. glacial lakes
c. moraines
d. wind erosions

Answer: a. The lithosphere is Earth's landforms.

• •

Answer: d. The Ring of Fire is an area of earthquake and volcanic activity that crosses continents and oceans.

• •

Answer: c. As glaciers melt and recede, they leave large piles of rock and debris known as moraines.

Fill in the blank with the correct term.

The Grand _____ was formed by water erosion.
a. Tsunami
b. Tetons
c. Canal
d. Canyon

· ·

Fill in the blank with the correct term.

Lines of _____, or parallels, circle Earth in degrees horizontally along the equator.
a. latitude
b. longitude
c. legend
d. meridians

· ·

Fill in the blank with the correct term.

Lines of longitude, or _____, circle Earth vertically from Pole to Pole.
a. meridians
b. prime meridians
c. international date lines
d. time zones

Answer: d. The Grand Canyon was formed by water erosion.

. . . .

Answer: a. Lines of latitude, or parallels, circle Earth in degrees horizontally along the equator.

. . . .

Answer: a. Lines of longitude, or meridians, circle Earth vertically from Pole to Pole.

GED® TEST SOCIAL STUDIES FLASH REVIEW

Fill in the blank with the correct term.

Southwest Asia, North Africa, and Central Asia are rich in

_____.

a. timber
b. water
c. produce
d. petroleum

. . . .

Fill in the blank with the correct term.

Indigenous North Africans preceding Arab invasions were

_____.

a. Maoris
b. Berbers
c. Bedouins
d. Ottoman Turks

. . . .

Fill in the blank with the correct term.

Judaism and Christianity were born in the _____.

a. Eastern Mediterranean
b. Arabian Peninsula
c. Sahel of North Africa
d. Central Asian steppe

Answer: d. Southwest Asia, North Africa, and Central Asia are rich in petroleum.

· ·

Answer: b. Indigenous North Africans preceding Arab invasions were Berbers.

· ·

Answer: a. Judaism and Christianity were born in the Eastern Mediterranean.

Fill in the blank with the correct term.

_____ largest agricultural floodplain surrounds the Ganges River.
a. India's
b. China's
c. Pakistan's
d. Nepal's

. . . .

Fill in the blank with the correct term.

The cities of Quebec, Montreal, and Ottawa developed along the _____.
a. Mississippi River
b. Great Plains
c. St. Lawrence River
d. Gulf of Mexico

. . . .

Fill in the blank with the correct term.

Since the 1970s, the mild climates of the American _____ and Southwest have attracted rapid population growth.
a. Midwest
b. Northeast
c. Rust Belt
d. South

Answer: a. India's largest agricultural floodplain surrounds the Ganges River.

. . . .

Answer: c. The cities of Quebec, Montreal, and Ottawa developed along the St. Lawrence River.

. . . .

Answer: d. Since the 1970s, the mild climates of the American South and Southwest have attracted rapid population growth.

Fill in the blank with the correct term.

The _____ climate zone of South America is coldest.
a. tierra helada
b. puna
c. tierra fria
d. tierra templada

· ·

Fill in the blank with the correct term.

The Olmec, Maya, Inca, Maori, Australian, Native American, and other indigenous tribes are also known as _____ cultures.
a. aboriginal
b. mestizo
c. machismo
d. Creole

· ·

Fill in the blank with the correct term.

The largest country in the world In size is _____.
a. Russia
b. China
c. India
d. Indonesia

Answer: a. The tierra helada climate zone of South America is coldest.

· ·

Answer: a. The Olmec, Maya, Inca, Maori, Australian, Native American, and other indigenous tribes are also known as aboriginal cultures.

· ·

Answer: a. The largest country in the world in size is Russia.

Fill in the blank with the correct term.

Ample coniferous forests make up Russia's largest climate zone, the _____.
a. tundra
b. subarctic
c. taiga
d. humid continental

· ·

Fill in the blank with the correct term.

Not including migration, negative population growth simply means _____.
a. the birth rate exceeds the death rate
b. the death rate exceeds the birth rate
c. the birth rate is not recorded
d. birth rate and death rates are equal

· ·

Fill in the blank with the correct term.

Glaciation formed the fjords of _____.
a. the Mediterranean
b. Scandinavia
c. canals
d. the North Sea

Answer: b. Ample coniferous forests make up Russia's largest climate zone, the subarctic.

....

Answer: b. Not including migration, negative population growth simply means the death rate exceeds the birth rate.

....

Answer: b. Glaciation formed the fjords of Scandinavia.

Fill in the blank with the correct term.

England, Wales, Scotland, and Northern Ireland make up _____.

a. the United Kingdom
b. the Celts
c. the British Isles
d. Great Britain

· ·

Fill in the blank with the correct term.

The _____ now combine(s) most of Europe into one economic community and conduct(s) more trade by volume than any country in the world.

a. North Atlantic Treaty Organization (NATO)
b. Organization of Petroleum Exporting Countries (OPEC)
c. European Union (EU)
d. guest workers

· ·

Fill in the blank with the correct term.

One positive response to deforestation is _____.

a. replanting trees and forests
b. expanding industrial use of coal
c. replanting trees and forests and expanding industrial use of coal
d. access to fossil fuel

Answer: a. England, Wales, Scotland, and Northern Ireland make up the United Kingdom.

. . . .

Answer: c. The European Union (EU) now combines most of Europe into one economic community and conducts more trade by volume than any country in the world.

. . . .

Answer: a. One positive response to deforestation is replanting trees and forests.

Fill in the blank with the correct term.

The edges of African plateaus are marked by steep, jagged cliffs called _____.

a. cataracts
b. escarpments
c. estuaries
d. kums

. . . .

Fill in the blank with the correct term.

South Africa has about half the world's _____.

a. rice
b. gold, diamonds, and uranium
c. spices
d. bat guano

. . . .

Fill in the blank with the correct term.

Large parts of Africa south of the Sahara currently face _____.

a. drought, famine, lack of clean water, inadequate sanitation, and epidemic disease
b. corruption, civil war, and human rights violations
c. drought, famine, lack of clean water, inadequate sanitation, epidemic disease, corruption, civil war, and human rights violations
d. tsunamis

Answer: b. The edges of African plateaus are marked by steep, jagged cliffs called escarpments.

· ·

Answer: b. South Africa has about half the world's gold, diamonds, and uranium.

· ·

Answer: c. Large parts of Africa south of the Sahara currently face drought, famine, lack of clean water, inadequate sanitation, and epidemic disease, as well as corruption, civil war, and human rights violations.

Fill in the blank with the correct term.

Independence from European rule came most recently in
_____.

a. Latin America
b. Asia
c. Africa
d. the Middle East

. . . .

Fill in the blank with the correct term.

Racial segregation in South Africa was called _____.
a. apartheid
b. Afrikaner
c. Zimbabwe
d. Angola

. . . .

Fill in the blank with the correct term.

Mount Fuji is in _____.
a. the Himalayas
b. China
c. Japan
d. Taiwan

Answer: c. Independence from European rule came most recently in Africa.

. . . .

Answer: a. Racial segregation in South Africa was called apartheid.

. . . .

Answer: c. Mount Fuji is in Japan.

Fill in the blank with the correct term.

The Himalayas separate China from _____.

a. Japan

b. Taiwan

c. South Asia

d. Mount Everest

. . . .

Fill in the blank with the correct term.

Seasonal monsoon winds help the major crop of _____ to grow in Southeast Asia's fertile paddies.

a. rice

b. wheat

c. corn

d. livestock

. . . .

Where is population density lowest?

a. China

b. Japan

c. Singapore

d. Mongolia

Answer: c. The Himalayas separate China from South Asia.

· ·

Answer: a. Seasonal monsoon winds help the major crop of rice to grow in Southeast Asia's fertile paddies.

· ·

Answer: d. Population density is the lowest in Mongolia.

GED® TEST SOCIAL STUDIES FLASH REVIEW

Fill in the blank with the correct term.

_____ is the world's most populous urban area, with more than 35 million people.
a. Beijing
b. Tokyo
c. Rio de Janiero
d. Shanghai

. . . .

Fill in the blank with the correct term.

Since 1945, Communist _____ Korea has sought to unify Korea and expand its nuclear capabilities.
a. North
b. South
c. West
d. East

. . . .

Fill in the blank with the correct term.

Over 60% of high-tech imports to the United States come from _____ Asia.
a. South
b. Southeast
c. East
d. Central

GED® TEST SOCIAL STUDIES FLASH REVIEW

Answer: b. Tokyo is the world's most populous urban area, with more than 35 million people.

. . . .

Answer: a. Since 1945, Communist North Korea has sought to unify Korea and expand its nuclear capabilities.

. . . .

Answer: c. Over 60% of high-tech imports to the United States come from East Asia.

Fill in the blank with the correct term.

The _____ Peninsula includes all of Vietnam, Laos, Cambodia, Myanmar, and part of Thailand.

a. Korean
b. Indochina
c. Hong Kong
d. Malay

. . . .

Fill in the blank with the correct term.

_____ cultivates over 1,000 species of orchids.

a. Thailand
b. Vietnam
c. Indonesia
d. Laos

. . . .

Fill in the blank with the correct term.

In the highland climate of Myanmar, you can find _____.

a. mangrove trees
b. cypress trees
c. rhododendrons
d. moss

Answer: b. The Indochina Peninsula includes all of Vietnam, Laos, Cambodia, Myanmar, and part of Thailand.

· ·

Answer: a. Thailand cultivates over 1,000 species of orchids.

· ·

Answer: c. In the highland climate of Myanmar, you can find rhododendrons.

Fill in the blank with the correct term.

_____ cities like Bangkok serve as a country's port, economic center, and often the capital.
a. Primate
b. Viceroyalty
c. Megalopolis
d. Animism

. . . .

Fill in the blank with the correct term.

The temple complex of Angkor Wat in Cambodia was influenced by _____.
a. Hinduism
b. Koryoism
c. Islam
d. Roman Catholicism

. . . .

Fill in the blank with the correct term.

Indonesia, Thailand, and Malaysia lead the world in _____ production.
a. tea
b. bamboo
c. rubber
d. petroleum

Answer: a. Primate cities like Bangkok serve as a country's port, economic center, and often the capital.

· ·

Answer: a. The temple complex of Angkor Wat in Cambodia was influenced by Hinduism.

· ·

Answer: c. Indonesia, Thailand, and Malaysia lead the world in rubber production.

Fill in the blank with the correct term.

Trawlers are used in commercial _____.
a. cattle ranching
b. rice farming
c. timber cutting
d. fishing

. . . .

Fill in the blank with the correct term.

The June 1991 volcanic eruption of Mount Pinatubo in _____ was one of the twentieth century's most violent and destructive volcanic eruptions.
a. Indonesia's island of Bali
b. Indonesia's island of Java
c. the Philippines
d. Japan

. . . .

Fill in the blank with the correct term.

The world's largest coral reef lies off the coast of _____.
a. New Zealand
b. South Africa
c. Australia
d. the United States

Answer: d. Trawlers are used in commercial fishing.

· ·

Answer: c. The June 1991 volcanic eruption of Mount Pinatubo in the Philippines was one of the twentieth century's most violent and destructive volcanic eruptions.

· ·

Answer: c. The world's largest coral reef lies off the coast of Australia.

Fill in the blank with the correct term.

Most animal life in Antarctica, such as whales, seals, and penguins, can be found _____.

a. in the Antarctic Ocean
b. in the Vinson Massif
c. in East Antarctica
d. at the South Pole

GED® TEST SOCIAL STUDIES FLASH REVIEW

Answer: a. Most animal life in Antarctica, such as whales, seals, and penguins, can be found in the Antarctic Ocean.

· ·

Look at the map, and then answer the following two questions.

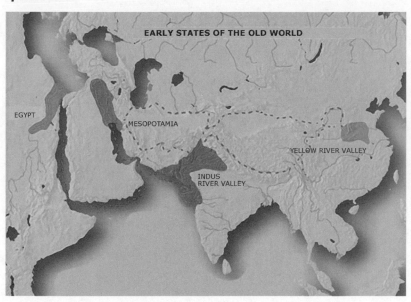

_____

Based on this map, which of the following can you conclude about ancient civilizations?
a. They grew along waterways.
b. They had stable governments.
c. They traded with one another.
d. They were located in cooler climates.

· ·

Which would be the best title for this map?
a. Ancient River Valley Civilizations
b. The Earliest Asian Cultures
c. Global Exploration and Trade
d. Rivers of the World

· ·

_____

Answer: a. As seen from the map, each of these civilizations grew along a waterway.

· ·

Answer: a. The map shows ancient civilizations that emerged along river valleys.

· ·

Use the maps to answer the following question.

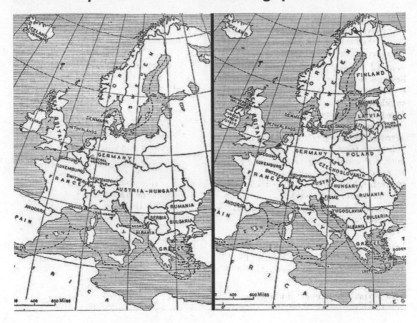

European boundaries changed radically after World War I. The map on the left shows the boundaries of European countries before World War I. The map on the right shows the boundaries of European countries after World War I.

Based on these two maps, all of the following changes took place during World War I *except*:

a. Poland was reestablished as an independent nation.
b. Serbia became part of Yugoslavia.
c. Germany increased its territory.
d. Poland had no outlet to the sea.

──────────

Answer: d. The Polish Corridor was created at the Treaty of Versailles to give Poland an outlet to the sea.

Use the illustration to answer the following two questions.

This illustration would be most helpful in writing a report about
a. England during the Industrial Revolution.
b. France in the Middle Ages.
c. Egypt under the Pharaohs.
d. China after the completion of the Great Wall.

· ·

Which feature of this illustration best indicates that warfare was common in this period?
a. Walls and a moat surround the town.
b. The cathedral is the largest building in the town.
c. Workers' sickles could easily be converted to military use.
d. The workers are well-dressed and seem to be laboring effortlessly.

· ·

———————

Answer: b. This type of castle wall with crenellations (as well as the cathedral with stained glass windows) is typical of medieval Europe, so France in the Middle Ages is the correct answer.

. . . .

Answer: a. Walls are usually built around a city only if someone or something needs to be kept out. Archaeologists and historians often use the presence or the absence of walls to determine the social setting of a city.

. . . .

The eighteenth-century slave trade was a "triangular" trade. A ship would travel from Europe to West Africa carrying cotton fabrics, hardware, and guns. In Africa, these items would be traded for slaves. The ship would then carry the slaves to the West Indies and the southern American colonies. Finally, the ship would return to Europe carrying sugar and tobacco.

Atlantic Slave Trade Routes

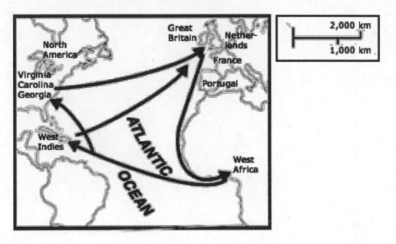

Which of the following would you most likely find on board an eighteenth-century ship sailing from the West Indies to Great Britain?

a. slaves
b. sugar
c. guns
d. textiles

GED® TEST SOCIAL STUDIES FLASH REVIEW

Answer: b. Ships sailing from the West Indies to Europe carried sugar and tobacco.

Which is the best conclusion that can be drawn from the information below?

"We are fighting for the liberty, the self-government, and the undictated development of all peoples. . . . No people must be forced under sovereignty under which it does not wish to live."

—Woodrow Wilson, 1917

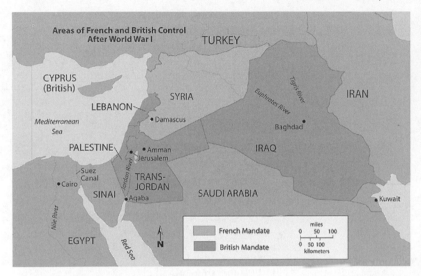

a. **The Treaty of Versailles honored the principle of self-determination for all peoples.**
b. **Arabs preferred to live under European rule after 1920.**
c. **U.S. influence was limited in the Middle East.**
d. **The collapse of the British Empire left a power vacuum in Trans-Jordan.**

Answer: c. This is the best conclusion based on the given information.

· ·

The following illustration is a six-panel folding screen with ink on paper drawn in the early 1500s by Soami (1472–1525), a famous Japanese painter. This part of a pair of screens depicting the seasons shows fall on the right and winter on the left.

Credit: The Metropolitan Museum of Art, Gift of John D. Rockefeller, Jr., 1941. Image © The Metropolitan Museum of Art.

A historian could use this screen to support which of the following positions?
a. Empty space is important in Japanese art.
b. Japan is a densely populated country.
c. Samurai used screen paintings to display their wealth.
d. Japanese art followed European traditions.

GED® TEST SOCIAL STUDIES FLASH REVIEW

Answer: a. The folding screen, known in Japanese as byobu, is one of the most distinctive and beautiful forms of Japanese art. Screens could serve as room partitions or settings for special events. They offered large surfaces to paint, and many of Japan's finest artists worked in this format. Large patches of unpainted space indicate that this choice is correct.

· ·

Use the map to answer the following question.

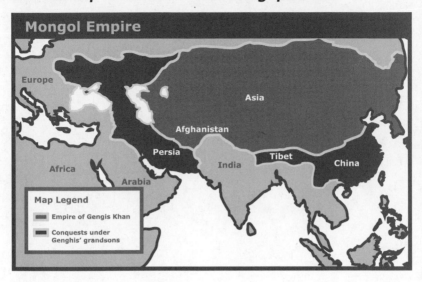

Mongol Empire

Europe

Asia

Afghanistan

Persia

Tibet

India

China

Africa

Arabia

Map Legend

Empire of Gengis Khan

Conquests under
Genghis' grandsons

The area conquered by Genghis Khan is best described as
a. **Persia.**
b. **Europe.**
c. **Arabia.**
d. **Central Asia.**

Answer: d. The map shows that Genghis Khan's conquests primarily cover the central part of the Asian continent.

Which conclusion can most fairly be drawn from this map?

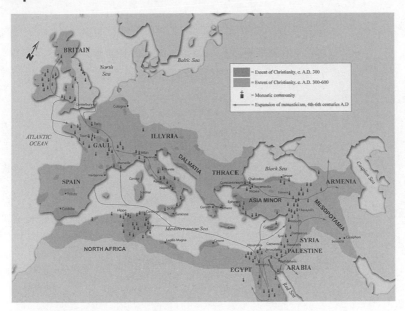

a. Christian armies conquered North Africa in the 200s.
b. Monastic communities were important in Spain.
c. The Crusades helped spread Christianity to the Holy Land.
d. Present-day Tunisia was a center of early monasticism.

Answer: d. Tunisia is located on the part of Africa closest to Italy.

· ·

What is the best conclusion based on the map and the poem?

"When in April the sweet showers fall And pierce the drought of March to the root. . . . Then people long to go on pilgrimages And pilgrims long to seek strange strands Of far-off shrines in distant lands."
—Geoffrey Chaucer, Prologue to *The Canterbury Tales* [c. 1380s]

Medieval Trade Routes in the Eleventh and Twelfth Centuries

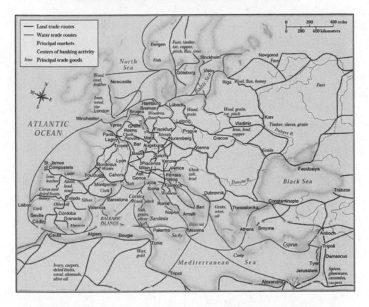

a. **Religious journeys involved travel to distant places.**
b. **Christians and Muslims avoided trading with each other.**
c. **Most medieval travel was for religious reasons.**
d. **People rarely traveled in the Middle Ages.**

Answer: a. This is a virtual paraphrase of Chaucer.

Use the maps and the information below to answer the following two questions.

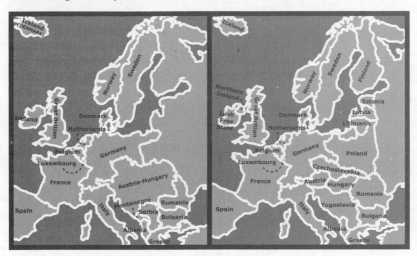

The maps above show the political borders of European nations before the start of World War I (the map on the left) and after the war concluded (the map on the right). At the end of World War I, Germany was required to sign the Treaty of Versailles, which required Germany to accept responsibility for causing the war. The treaty also required Germany to pay the victor nations over 6 million pounds in reparations and to cede some of its land, including its valuable coal mines on the German-French border. In addition, Germany had to give up all of her colonies, which had provided her with a steady source of income. Finally, strict limitations were placed on the size and weaponry of the German military, and the country was forbidden from entering into an alliance with neighboring Austria.

Which country increased in size at the conclusion of World War I?
a. **Austria-Hungary**
b. **Norway**
c. **Rumania (Romania)**
d. **Ireland**

Answer: c. Of the countries listed, only Rumania increased in size, according to the maps.

Which of the following is a FACT about the Treaty of Versailles?
a. The Treaty of Versailles harmed the German economy.
b. Germany deserved the harsh terms of the treaty because Germany started the war.
c. If the Treaty of Versailles had been fairer to Germany, the Nazis never would have gained power.
d. The United States was the country that benefited the most from the Treaty of Versailles.

. . . .

In the early 1960s, an independence movement swept across Africa. In just a few years, colonies of European nations, such as France, the United Kingdom, and Belgium, became independent nations with constitutions and free elections. This movement was a clear expression of the philosophy of
a. Divine Rights.
b. Natural Rights.
c. Manifest Destiny.
d. Religious Zealotry.

. . . .

According to some analysts, a temperate climate is most conducive to human productivity. Which of the following would be the best evidence to support this claim?
a. Many areas of the temperate region are rich in natural resources.
b. Tropical regions are most attractive to tourists and vacationers.
c. The world's five largest economies are all located in the temperate region.
d. The most severe damage from the two world wars was in the temperate region.

Answer: a. According to the passage, the Treaty of Versailles imposed huge fines on Germany and stripped the country of valuable property. These provisions harmed the German economy by depriving it of cash and income, which it needed to rebuild the country after an extremely costly war. Each of the incorrect choices is an opinion, not a fact.

. . . .

Answer: b. This movement was a clear expression of the philosophy of Natural Rights. The philosophy of Natural Rights claims that the right to rule comes from the people. Transferring political power from a foreign colonial power to an elected local government would be a real-life example of the philosophy of Natural Rights. Divine Rights is a philosophy that proposes the right to rule comes from a connection with God, or a "divine" power.

. . . .

Answer: c. According to some analysts, the fact that the world's five largest economies are all located in the temperate region offers strong evidence that a temperate climate is most conducive to human productivity.

Which of the following predictions is best supported by the world population growth data in the chart?

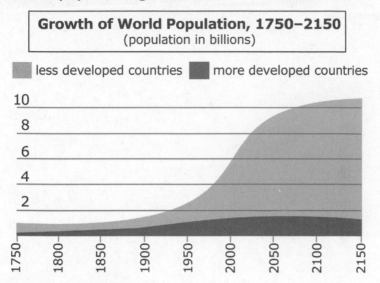

Growth of World Population, 1750–2150
(population in billions)

less developed countries   more developed countries

a. **The world population growth rate will be declining starting by 2050.**
b. **The less developed countries will continue to grow rapidly for the next 150 years.**
c. **The developed countries will experience a population collapse in the next century.**
d. **Within the next century, world population will level off and begin to decline.**

· ·

Answer: a. That the world population growth rate will be declining by 2050 is the prediction best supported by the graph. While the total population continues to increase, the slope of the line, or rate of growth, is decreasing.

Use the map to answer the following question.

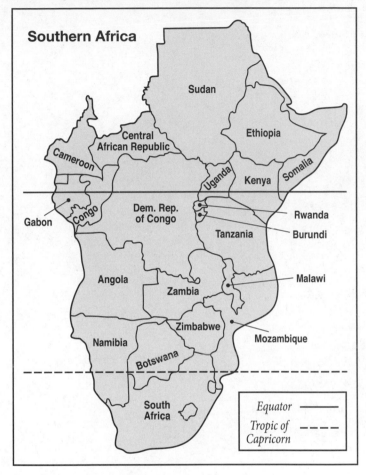

Southern Africa

Which countries lie entirely between the Tropic of Capricorn and the Equator?
a. Namibia and Botswana
b. Angola and Malawi
c. South Africa and Kenya
d. Angola and South Africa

GED® TEST SOCIAL STUDIES FLASH REVIEW

———————————

Answer: b. Among the choices, the only two countries listed that lie entirely between the Tropic of Capricorn and the Equator are Angola and Malawi.

Which countries belong to OPEC but not to the Arab League or ASEAN?

International Organization	Members
Arab League	Algeria, Bahrain, Comoros, Djibouti, Egypt, Iraq, Jordan, Kuwait, Lebanon, Libya, Mauritania, Morocco, Oman, Qatar, Saudi Arabia, Somalia, Sudan, Syria, Tunisia, United Arab Emirates, Yemen, Palestine Liberation Organization
Organization of Petroleum Exporting Countries (OPEC)	Algeria, Angola, Ecuador, Iran, Iraq, Kuwait, Libya, Nigeria, Qatar, Saudi Arabia, United Arab Emirates, Venezuela
Association of Southeast Asian Nations (ASEAN)	Brunei, Cambodia, Indonesia, Laos, Malaysia, Myanmar, Philippines, Singapore, Thailand, Vietnam

a. **Brunei and Myanmar**
b. **Iran and Iraq**
c. **Qatar and United Arab Emirates**
d. **Nigeria and Venezuela**

. . . .

Answer: d. These are the only countries that belong to OPEC but not to the Arab League or ASEAN.

Use the chart and quote to answer the following two questions.

Foreign Trade of the United States
(in Millions of U.S. Dollars)

Year	Exports	Imports
1860	400	362
1870	451	462
1880	853	761
1890	910	823
1900	1,499	930
1910	1,919	1,646
1920	8,664	5,784

"The Philippines are ours forever. . . . And just beyond the Philippines are China's illimitable [limitless] markets. We will not retreat from either. . . . We will not abandon our opportunity in the Orient. We will not renounce our part in the mission of our race, trustee under God, of the civilization of the world. The Pacific is our ocean. . . . Where shall we turn for consumers of our surplus? Geography answers the question. China is our natural customer. . . . The Philippines give us a base at the door of all the East. . . . No land in America surpasses in fertility the plains and valleys of Luzon. Rice and coffee, sugar and coconuts, hemp and tobacco. . . ."
—Albert Beveridge, U.S. Senator from Indiana, January 9, 1900

Based on his comments, all of the following factors contributed to Senator Beveridge's desire to annex the Philippines, except
a. he believed in the wealth of the Philippines.
b. he wanted better access to China.
c. he opposed economic imperialism.
d. he believed people to be less civilized.

_____

Answer: c. Beveridge is giving the classic justification for economic imperialism.

. . . .

What is the most likely reason for the Allied retreat of November 26?

First Phase of the Korean Conflict, 1950

June 25 — North Korea invades South Korea.

June 27 — The UN asks member nations to aid South Korea.

July 1 — Allied troops from the US and other UN members begin arriving in South Korea.

October 19 — Allied troops capture Pyongyang, the North Korean capital.

October 25 — China enters the war on the side of North Korea.

November 26 — Allied troops begin to retreat.

a. **The arrival of Chinese troops greatly increased enemy strength.**
b. **Chinese forces withdrew from the Korean peninsula.**
c. **The UN called for a general end to the conflict.**
d. **The capture of Pyongyang was the only goal of the Allied alliance.**

Answer: a. The proximity in time between China's entering the conflict and the retreat of Allied troops suggests that China's entrance into the war was the cause for the Allied retreat.

As damaging as it was in terms of American lives lost, World War II had an even greater effect on the lives of British, French, and Soviet soldiers and civilians. This chart compares the losses.

Country	Military Losses	Civilian Losses
United States	292,131	fewer than 10
Britain	397,762	70,000
France	210,671	173,260
Soviet Union	14,500,000	7,700,000

Which of the following most likely explains why civilian losses were so much lower in the United States than in Europe?
a. The U.S. military was better able to protect its civilians.
b. Outside of certain Alaskan islands, no fighting took place on U.S. soil.
c. U.S. civilians were not allowed to witness battles.
d. More U.S. civilians were drafted into the armed forces.

· ·

Answer: b. During World War II, no fighting took place on U.S. soil except in the Aleutian Islands off Alaska. No battles took place in Great Britain either, but British soldiers fought in the major battles in Europe. So did French and Soviet soldiers, and all these countries suffered civilian losses from German bombing and/or occupation.

A civil war is defined as a war between factions or regions of the same country. Based on this definition, which of these is NOT a civil war?
a. the 1642 struggle between supporters of the king and parliamentarians in England
b. the 1918 conflict between the anticommunist White Army and the Red Army of the Soviets in Russia
c. the war between the Hutu and Tutsi peoples in present-day Rwanda
d. the 1904 conflict between Russia and Japan over control of Manchuria and Korea

. . . .

Please use the chart to answer the following question.

Famous Explorers of the Middle Ages

Name	Nationality	Journeys	Date
Eric the Red	Norwegian	to Greenland from Iceland	c. 982
Leif Ericsson	Norwegian	may have reached mainland North America	c. 1000
Marco Polo	Italian	Sri Lanka, China, India, Iran, Sumatra	1271–1295
Odoric of Pordenone	Italian	Turkey, Iran, across Central Asia, Indian and South Pacific oceans	c. 1314–c. 1330

Which of the following most likely explains why the Norwegian explorers traveled west whereas the Italian explorers traveled east?
a. The Italians were looking for wealth, but the Norwegians were looking for land.
b. Geography made it easier to travel eastward from Italy and westward from Norway.
c. Italian explorers had already visited North America.
d. Norwegian explorers had nothing to trade with the people of Asia.

. . . .

Answer: d. The only conflict between two different countries is the one between Russia and Japan.

. . . .

_____

Answer: b. The difference in the geography of these two countries most likely explains why Norwegians sailed west and Italians sailed east.

. . . .

Use the chart below to answer the following three questions.

The Neolithic Era saw significant climatic changes that allowed for the beginning of farming in many parts of the world.

The Rise of Farming in the Neolithic Era

9000 B.C.	collection of wild cereals, domestication of dog, pig, goat
8000 B.C.	cereal cultivation, first villages, pottery, cattle-keeping groups
7000 B.C.	linen textiles, copper ornaments, root crops, domestication of sheep and cattle
6000 B.C.	smelting, irrigation, plowing
5000 B.C.	woolen textiles, domestication of horse and donkey, tree crops, maize, rice cultivation
4000 B.C.	domestication of llama by New World peoples, cotton textiles, wheeled vehicles, sailboats

How did people's lives change when they began cultivating cereal crops?
a. They stopped being afraid of wild animals.
b. They started painting on the walls of caves.
c. They started using fire to cook their food.
d. They started settling down in villages.

_____

Answer: d. According to the time line, the cultivation of cereal crops occurred around 8000 B.C. At that time, the most significant development was the appearance of villages in which people settled.

Is it reasonable to conclude that cattle were used for plowing before horses were?

a. No, because horses were domesticated before cattle were.
b. No, because cattle were still wild when plowing was introduced.
c. Yes, because horses were not yet domesticated when plowing was introduced.
d. Yes, because cattle were more common than horses were.

. . . .

Which statement based on the diagram is an opinion rather than a fact?

a. The wheel was invented long after people settled down in villages.
b. Dugout canoes preceded sailboats by thousands of years.
c. Olive trees and fruit trees were first cultivated around 5000 B.C.
d. Irrigation was the Neolithic era's most important innovation.

. . . .

Answer: c. The time line makes it clear that plowing occurred before the domestication of the horse, so it is reasonable to conclude that cattle were used for plowing.

. . . .

Answer: d. Choice d is the only opinion among the five choices. The words *most important* give a clue that the statement is a value judgment, not a fact.

. . . .

GED® TEST SOCIAL STUDIES FLASH REVIEW

Use the map to answer the following question.

Portuguese Sea Routes to the East

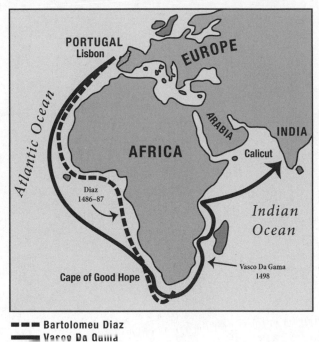

- ■■■ Bartolomeu Diaz
- ■■■ Vasco Da Gama

Based on the map, Portuguese explorer Bartolomeu Diaz, on his voyage of 1486–87

a. purchased spices and jewels in India and brought them back to Portugal.

b. proved the existence of a sea route around southern Africa to the Indian Ocean.

c. managed to reach Calicut in India in only two years.

d. circled the globe and proved once and for all that the world was round.

. . . .

GED® TEST SOCIAL STUDIES FLASH REVIEW

Answer: b. The map shows that Diaz sailed south from Portugal, rounded the southern tip of Africa, and entered the Indian Ocean. This choice is the only conclusion that can fairly be drawn from the information in the map: Diaz's voyage proved that there is a sea route around southern Africa to the Indian Ocean.

"The history of the world is the record of a man in quest of his daily bread and butter."

—Hendrik Willem van Loon

_____

Which of these methods of looking at history would van Loon find most valuable?
a. gender studies
b. historical geography
c. autobiography
d. economic history

. . . .

What do the Loire and Garonne rivers have in common?
a. They both flow from west to east.
b. They both flow from north to south.
c. They both empty into the Atlantic Ocean.
d. They both empty into the Mediterranean Sea.

. . . .

_____

Answer: d. The quotation implies that the most important aspect of history is economic history, "the record of man in quest of his daily bread and butter."

· ·

Answer: c. The map shows that the Loire and Garonne rivers both flow into the Atlantic Ocean.

· ·

Please use the table to answer the following question.

International Organization	Members
Arab League	Algeria, Bahrain, Comoros, Djibouti, Egypt, Iraq, Jordan, Kuwait, Lebanon, Libya, Mauritania, Morocco, Oman, Qatar, Saudi Arabia, Somalia, Sudan, Syria, Tunisia, United Arab Emirates, Yemen, Palestine Liberation Organization
Organization of Petroleum Exporting Countries (OPEC)	Algeria, Indonesia, Iran, Iraq, Kuwait, Libya, Nigeria, Qatar, Saudi Arabia, United Arab Emirates, Venezuela
Association of Southeast Asian Nations (ASEAN)	Brunei, Burma, Cambodia, Indonesia, Laos, Malaysia, Philippines, Singapore, Thailand, Vietnam

Which country belongs to OPEC and ASEAN but not the Arab League?
a. **Indonesia**
b. **Algeria**
c. **Iraq**
d. **Kuwait**

—————————

Answer: a. The only country that belongs to OPEC and ASEAN but not to the Arab League is Indonesia.

· ·

Earliest Civilizations

	Egypt	Sumer	India	China
Start Date	3000 B.C.	3200 B.C.	2500 B.C.	2100 B.C.
Location	Nile River valley	Euphrates River valley (Iraq)	Indus River valley	Huang Ho River valley
Main Sites	Memphis, Thebes	Ur, Eridu	Harappa, Mohenjo-Daro	Zhengzhou, Anyang
Types of Writing	hieroglyphics	cuneiform	Indus writing	Chinese characters
Forms of Government	monarchy	monarchy	unknown	monarchy

Which conclusion is best supported by the information presented in the chart?

a. All early civilizations were monarchies.

b. Egypt is the oldest of the world's civilizations.

c. Many of the world's earliest civilizations developed in river valleys.

d. All early civilizations used a type of writing called hieroglyphics.

—————

Answer: c. Many of the world's earliest civilizations developed in river valleys.

· ·

Which of the following conclusions can you make from the chart?

African-American Slaves in the United States, 1790–1860

Year	Northern States		Southern States	
	Free	Slave	Free	Slave
1790	27,034	40,086	32,523	657,538
1800	47,196	36,505	64,239	857,097
1810	78,181	25,510	108,265	1,163,852
1820	99,307	19,108	134,327	1,518,914
1830	137,529	3,568	182,070	2,005,475
1840	170,728	1,129	215,565	2,486,226
1850	196,208	262	238,187	3,204,051
1860	226,152	64	261,918	3,953,696

a. **Slavery became a greater part of the economy of the South than of the North.**
b. **Slaves lived a more difficult life in the South than in the North.**
c. **More slaves in the North fought for their freedom.**
d. **About one of every five African Americans was free by 1860.**

Answer: a. The statistics show that slavery became a part of the southern economy.

· ·

Use the map to answer the following two questions.

The Expansion of Islam, 600 to 750 C.E.

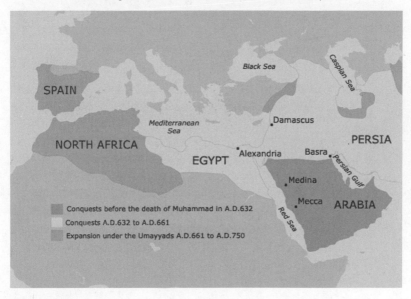

During the time on the map, the Islam religion had expanded to encompass the entire area of all of the modern-day countries *except*

a. Portugal.
b. Saudi Arabia.
c. Turkey.
d. Iraq.

_____

Answer: c. Parts of modern-day Turkey remained under Byzantine Christian control until 1453. The map shows that the other four nations had been conquered by 750 C.E.

Based on this map, which of the following conclusions is most reasonable?

a. The Mediterranean Sea ceased to be an important trade route in the Middle Ages.
b. Islam expanded outward from its starting place in Egypt.
c. No part of Europe was ever occupied by an Islamic army.
d. Christian control of the Mediterranean coast of North Africa had ceased by 750.

. . . .

Read the passage below and answer the following question.

The eighteenth-century slave trade was a "triangular" trade. A ship would travel from Europe to West Africa carrying cotton fabrics, hardware, and guns. In Africa, these items would be traded for slaves. The ship would then carry the slaves to the West Indies and the southern American colonies. Finally, the ship would return to Europe carrying sugar and tobacco.

_____

Which of the following would you most likely find on board an eighteenth-century slave ship sailing from the West Indies to Great Britain?

a. slaves
b. cotton fabrics
c. sugar
d. guns

. . . .

Answer: d. This is the only choice illustrated on the map.

· ·

Answer: c. Ships sailing from the West Indies to Europe carried sugar and tobacco.

· ·

Use the graphs below to answer the following three questions.

World Population Growth Rate: 1950–2050

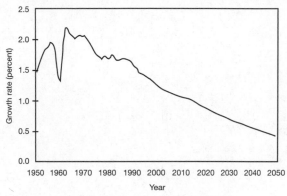

Rate of population growth = birth rate – death rate

Source: U.S. Census Bureau, International Data Base 10-2002.

World Population: 1950–2050

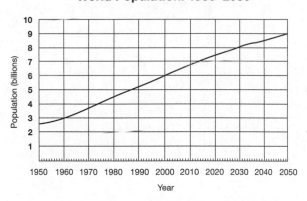

Source: U.S. Census Bureau, International Data Base 10-2002.

_____

The greatest increase in the population growth rate between 1950 and 2000 occurred in
a. 2001–2002.
b. 2000–2001.
c. 1990–2000.
d. 1962–1963.

Answer: d. The first graph shows the highest point in population growth rate between 1962 and 1963.

The world population growth rate dropped one percentage point between the mid-1950s and 1960. Which of the following best explains this occurrence?
a. The ratio of births to deaths was higher in the mid-1950s than it was in 1960.
b. A baby boom in the decade after World War II caused a spike in the birth rate.
c. The introduction of the birth control pill in 1960 in the United States helped to slow the birth rate.
d. There were more births in 1960 than there were in the mid-1950s.

. . . .

Which of the following statements is proved by the information in the two graphs?
a. The population will reach its limit by 2050.
b. When the rate of population growth decreases, so does the population.
c. When the rate of population growth increases, so does the population.
d. Even though the rate of population growth is decreasing, the population is increasing.

. . . .

Answer: a. The population growth rate increases when the ratio of births to deaths increases.

. . . .

Answer: d. Using the two graphs, you can compare the rate of population growth with the growth of the population. The growth rate is decreasing, while the population is increasing.

. . . .

In 150 A.D. the Greek astronomer Ptolemy taught that the solar system was structured as shown in Figure 1. Much later, in the 16th century, the Polish astronomer Nicolai Copernicus proposed the structure shown in Figure 2.

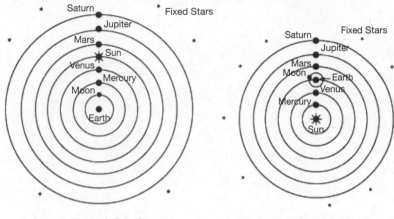

Figure 1. Ptolemy's Solar System   Figure 2. Copernicus's Solar System

The biggest difference between Ptolemy's and Copernicus's ideas is
a. Ptolemy thought that Mars and Venus were comets, but Copernicus said they were planets.
b. Ptolemy thought that Earth was at the center of the solar system, but Copernicus said that the sun was at the center.
c. Ptolemy thought that Saturn was the most distant planet, but Copernicus said that there was another planet beyond Saturn.
d. Ptolemy thought that the orbits of the planets were circular, but Copernicus said they were oval in shape.

Answer: b. It is the only statement that is true about the Ptolemaic and Copernican views of the solar system.

· ·

Which conclusion is best supported by the information presented in the chart?

Earliest Civilizations

	Egypt	Sumer	India	China
Start Date	3000 B.C.	3200 B.C.	2500 B.C.	2100 B.C.
Location	Nile River valley	Euphrates River valley (Iraq)	Indus River valley	Huang Ho River valley
Main Sites	Memphis, Thebes	Ur, Eridu	Harappa, Mohenjo-Daro	Zhengzhou, Anyang
Types of Writing	hieroglyphics	cuneiform	Indus writing	Chinese characters
Forms of Government	monarchy	monarchy	unknown	monarchy

a. All early civilizations were monarchies.
b. China is the oldest of the world's civilizations.
c. Many of the world's earliest civilizations developed in river valleys.
d. Civilization began in China and spread westward across Asia.

Answer: c. This is the only statement that is true.

. . . .

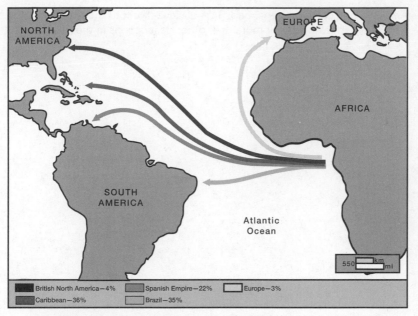

British North America—4%   Spanish Empire—22%   Europe—3%

Caribbean—36%   Brazil—35%

Source: Data derived from Hugh Thomas, *The Slave Trade*. Simon & Schuster, 1997.

According to the information given in the map, which of the following conclusions can be drawn?

a. The British colonies were the main destination of African slaves.

b. South America did not allow the importation of slaves.

c. Most slaves were sent to work on sugar plantations in Brazil and in the Caribbean.

d. South America has a large population of African origin today.

. . . .

Answer: c. According to the map, 36% of slaves went to the Caribbean and 35% went to Brazil, far more than other destinations in the Americas.

Use the map to answer the following question.

Ancient Egypt

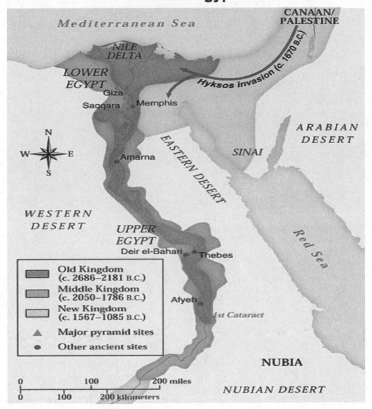

Credit: *The Making of the West*, Vol. 1: to 1740, by Lynn Hunt et al., Copyright © 2001 by Bedford/St. Martin's. Reproduced by permission of Bedford/St. Martin's.

Which conclusion can most fairly be drawn from the map?
a. Egyptian civilization predated Chinese civilization.
b. More than two-thirds of Egypt's population lived along the Mediterranean Sea.
c. The Nile Delta was one of the last areas settled by the Egyptians.
d. Palestine served as a potential route for Asian invasion into Africa.

Answer: c. The Hyksos were among the first of several invaders to attack Africa through Palestine.

Which conclusion can most fairly be drawn from the following chart?

Approximate First Production of Paper

Location	Date
China	105 C.E.
Uzbekistan	751
Egypt	900
Italy	1276
France	1348
England	1495

a. **The Chinese successfully prevented the spread of paper for more than 600 years.**
b. **The Chinese had no use for paper, so they sold the formula to the Uzbeks.**
c. **Medieval Europe was technologically superior to anywhere else in the world.**
d. **Paper was produced in England more than a millennium after its production in China.**

Answer: d. According to the chart, paper was first produced in China. The information on the chart will not, by itself, substantiate any of the other conclusions.

Read the passage and answer the following two questions.

Mohandas Gandhi, also known as Mahatma Gandhi, developed a policy of passive resistance in his civil rights struggle for Indian immigrants in South Africa and later in the campaign for Indian independence from British rule. The writings of the Russian author Leo Tolstoy and the essay "Civil Disobedience" by nineteenth-century American Henry David Thoreau inspired Gandhi. Gandhi called acts of nonviolent resistance *satyagraha*, a Sanskrit term meaning "truth and firmness." The Salt Satyagraha of 1930 exemplified his policy. In protest to the British government's salt tax, Gandhi led tens of thousands of Indians on a 200-mile march to the Arabian Sea, where they made salt from evaporated sea water. Thousands, including Gandhi, were arrested. When the British conceded to his demands, Gandhi stopped the campaign. When he was released from prison in 1931, he traveled to London as a representative of the Indian National Congress to negotiate reform measures.

Which of the following would be the best title for this passage?
a. **The Salt March of 1930**
b. **How to Lead an Effective Protest**
c. **Gandhi's Acts of Nonviolent Resistance**
d. **Free India**

. . . .

Which of the following conclusions can be drawn from the passage?
a. **Gandhi's nonviolent protests were effective political tools.**
b. **The British did not respond to the Salt Satyagraha.**
c. **Satyagraha means "truth and firmness" in Sanskrit.**
d. **Gandhi refused to support the British government in World War II until it granted India its independence.**

. . . .

———————

Answer: c. Choice c is general enough to encompass the main ideas of the passage.

. . . .

Answer: a. The British concession to Gandhi's demands shows that his use of nonviolent protest was an effective political tool.

. . . .

Use the chart to answer the following two questions.

Country	Number of Jews in 1937	Number of Jews in 1945
Poland	3,300,000	300,000
Soviet Union	3,020,000	1,920,000
Hungary	800,000	204,000
Germany	566,000	366,000
France	350,000	273,000
Romania	342,000	55,000
Netherlands	140,000	40,000

Which statement best explains the statistics on the chart?
a. The Nazi government carried out a program to exterminate Jews.
b. The accuracy of census counts was undermined by World War II.
c. Most Jews moved to Israel during World War II.
d. After 1940, census takers did not ask residents about religion.

. . . .

What would be the best title for this chart?
a. European Race and Ethnicity
b. Mass Migration
c. The Holocaust
d. A Decade of Homicide

. . . .

Answer: a. This is the only possible answer based on the statistics in the chart.

· ·

Answer: c. *Genocide* is the deliberate and systematic attempt to destroy a racial, religious, national, or ethnic group. The word was first used in 1944 in relation to the German attempt to exterminate the Jews of Europe.

· ·

What is the main idea of the following cartoon?

a. The League of Nations failed to work even after the United States joined it.

b. Most people in the United States wanted the League of Nations to fail.

c. The U.S. Congress saved the country from involvement in the affairs of Europe.

d. Public opinion in the United States opposed the Treaty of Versailles.

Answer: c. This is the correct answer. The cartoonist clearly feels that the Senate—carrying its *constitutional rights*—is within its rights in objecting to Uncle Sam's involvement in *foreign entanglements* (on the bride's dress).

Credit: The Metropolitan Museum of Art, The Michael C. Rockefeller Memorial Collection, Gift of Nelson A. Rockefeller, 1965. Image © The Metropolitan Museum of Art.

The kingdom of Benin, in the area around present-day Nigeria, produced remarkable brass (often called *bronze* by Europeans) artwork from the twelfth century to the seventeenth century. On this plaque, the king (*oba*) rides sidesaddle. He is supported by the hands of two servants and protected from the sun by their shields.

———————

Based on this bronze, which conclusion can be made most fairly?
a. Draft animals were nonexistent in West Africa.
b. West Africans understood principles of metallurgy.
c. Benin artists did not comprehend the difference between bronze and brass.
d. Civilization in Benin was far more advanced than in the rest of West Africa.

[401]

_____

Answer: b. _Metallurgy_ relates to the science and technology of working with metals and alloys. Benin artists knew what they were doing.

Use the chart to answer the following question.

Population of Top Ten U.S. Cities in 1790

Rank	City
1	Philadelphia, PA
2	New York, NY
3	Boston, MA
4	Charleston, SC
5	Baltimore, MD
6	Salem, MA
7	Newport, RI
8	Providence, RI
9	Marblehead, MA
10	Portsmouth, NH

How would a list of today's top ten cities compare to this list from 1790?

a. **All of the cities listed would be the same.**

b. **Some of the cities would be the same, but the list would include cities in the South and West.**

c. **Some of the cities would be the same, but there would be more cities in New England.**

d. **None of the cities would be the same.**

_____

Answer: b. In 1790, the United States extended only as far as the Mississippi River, and the largest cities hugged the Atlantic Coast. Today's population has moved west and south.

· ·

Read the passage and answer the following two questions.

From 2000 B.C. until the twentieth century, a succession of dynasties ruled China. The word *China* comes from the Ch'in Dynasty (221–206 B.C.), which first unified the country by conquering warring land-owning feudal lords. King Cheng named himself Shih Huang-ti, or first emperor, and consolidated his empire by abolishing feudal rule, creating a centralized monarchy, establishing a system of laws and a common written language, and building roads and canals to the capital. Scholars speculate that construction of the Great Wall or *chang cheng*, meaning "long wall," began during the Ch'in Dynasty in order to protect China's northern border from invaders. Shih Huang-ti ruled with absolute power, imposing strict laws and heavy taxes and doling out harsh punishments. He also is reputed to have burned books on topics that he did not consider useful. Shih Huang-ti died in 210 B.C. His son succeeded him but soon peasants and former nobles revolted and overthrew the dynasty. The Han Dynasty replaced it, ruling China until A.D. 220.

_____

Which of the following is NOT a contribution of the Ch'in Dynasty?
a. unification of territory
b. feudal aristocracy
c. road construction
d. standardized written script

. . . .

Which of the following conclusions can you make based on the passage?
a. The Ch'in Dynasty enjoyed a stable and long-lasting rule.
b. By abolishing feudalism, Ch'in Shih Huang-ti promoted democracy in China.
c. The Ch'in Dynasty was popular among peasants and displaced nobles.
d. The Ch'in Dynasty had long-lasting influence.

. . . .

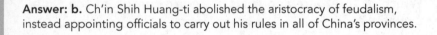

Answer: b. Ch'in Shih Huang-ti abolished the aristocracy of feudalism, instead appointing officials to carry out his rules in all of China's provinces.

· ·

Answer: d. The Ch'in Dynasty introduced a centralized government ruled by a monarchy—a form of government that lasted in China until 1911, when revolutionaries overthrew the last dynasty.

· ·

Read the passage and answer the following question.

Machu Picchu is an ancient stone city situated on a mountain ridge high in the Peruvian Andes, above the Sacred Valley. The Incas built the city around 1450, at the height of their empire. The city follows a strict plan in which agricultural and residential areas are separated by a large square. Most archeologists believe that Machu Picchu served as a religious and ceremonial center of the Incan Empire.

The Incas chose Machu Picchu for its unique location and features. Getting to Machu Picchu requires a journey up a narrow path. This makes it easily defended, as no one could approach without being spotted.

Machu Picchu was abandoned shortly after Spanish conquistadors vanquished the Incan Empire. Over the next several centuries, the jungle reclaimed the site on which Machu Picchu lay. The site was once again "discovered" by an American historian and explorer in 1911. Since then, archeologists have flocked to the site to see what they can learn about the Incas. Today, Machu Picchu—the Lost City of the Incas—is the most visited site in Peru.

———————

Which hypothesis is supported by the evidence in this passage?

a. The Incas would have expanded their empire had Columbus not discovered the Americas.
b. If Machu Picchu had not been discovered in 1911, we would not know anything about the Incas.
c. Machu Picchu would have survived many more years had Columbus not discovered the Americas.
d. If the Incas had built fortified centers on lower ground, they would have been able to beat the Conquistadors.

Answer: c. This is the only hypothesis that is supported by evidence from the passage. Columbus's discovery led to the Spanish conquest of the New World and the decline of the Incan Empire.

Read the passage and answer the following question.

German printer Johannes Gutenberg is often credited with the invention of the first printing press to use movable type. He used hand-set type to print the Gutenberg Bible in 1455. Although his invention greatly influenced printing in Europe, similar technologies were used earlier in China and Korea. Chinese printers used movable block prints and type made of clay as early as 1040, and Korean printers invented movable copper type about 1392.

———————————

What is the purpose of the paragraph?
a. to praise the advances of printing technology
b. to connect the early advances in printing with today's technological advances
c. to show that technological advances can develop in different geographical areas over periods of time
d. to give credit to Gutenberg for the first movable-type printing press

---

Answer: c. Although Gutenberg is given credit for the invention of movable type, others in different parts of the world at different time periods had used a similar technique. This does not lessen the great effect that Gutenberg's invention had on European culture.

· ·

Read the passage and answer the following three questions.

Even though acid rain looks, feels, and even tastes like clean rainwater, it contains high levels of pollutants. Scientists believe car exhaust and smoke from factories and power plants are the main causes of acid rain, but natural sources like gases from forest fires and volcanoes may also contribute to the problem. Pollutants mix in the atmosphere to form fine particles that can be carried long distances by wind. Eventually they return to the ground in the form of rain, snow, fog, or other precipitation. Acid rain damages trees and causes the acidification of lakes and streams, contaminating drinking water and damaging aquatic life. It erodes buildings, paint, and monuments. It can also affect human health. Although acid rain does not directly harm people, high levels of the fine particles in acid rain are linked to an increased risk for asthma and bronchitis. Since the 1950s, the increase of acid rain has become a problem in the northeastern United States, Canada, and western Europe. Some believe it is the single greatest industrial threat to the environment, although most feel that the emission of greenhouse gases is a far larger problem.

Which of the following natural resources is least likely to be affected by acid rain?
a. animal life
b. plant life
c. coal reserves
d. water

. . . .

Which of the following is NOT a cause of acid rain?
a. human activity
b. natural phenomena
c. volcanoes
d. lakes and streams

. . . .

Answer: c. All of these natural resources are negatively affected by acid rain except coal reserves. The passage identifies coal burning as a source of acid rain. It does not say that coal reserves are harmed by acid rain.

. . . .

Answer: d. Lakes and streams are affected by acid rain but do not cause it.

. . . .

Which of the following is an OPINION stated in the passage?

a. Acid rain is formed when pollutants mix in the atmosphere.

b. Acid rain damages trees, lakes, and streams.

c. Acid rain cannot be distinguished from unpolluted rain by sight, smell, or taste.

d. No industrial pollutant causes more damage to the environment than acid rain.

. . . .

Use the map to answer the following four questions.

Roman Conquest of Gaul (Gallia), 58–51 B.C.

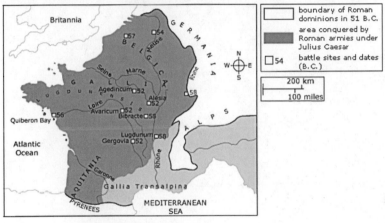

A battle took place along what river in 54 B.C.?

a. Rhine

b. Seine

c. Meuse

d. Marne

. . . .

Answer: d. Only choice d is an opinion; it draws a comparison that can be reasonably argued. In fact, the passage notes that choice d is the subject of some debate. According to the final sentence of the passage, many people believe that greenhouse gas emissions, not acid rain, are the greatest source of concern.

Answer: c. According to the map of the Roman conquest of Gaul, a battle took place in 54 B.C. along the Meuse River in the region then called Belgica.

Which of the following lists battles in order from earliest to latest?
a. Gergovia, Quiberon Bay, Lugdunum
b. Alesia, Lugdunum, Quiberon Bay
c. Quiberon Bay, Agedincum, Bibracte
d. Bibracte, Quiberon Bay, Gergovia

. . . .

Which conclusion is best supported by the information presented in the map?
a. The Romans conquered Aquitania and Belgica.
b. The Romans began their war of conquest in the north and worked their way south.
c. The battle at Lugdunum lasted several months.
d. Following the conquest of Gaul, the Romans planned to cross the Pyrenees.

. . . .

What do the Loire and Garonne rivers have in common?
a. They both flow from west to east.
b. They both flow from north to south.
c. They both empty into the Atlantic Ocean.
d. They both empty into the Mediterranean Sea.

Answer: d. According to the map of the Roman conquest of Gaul, various battles were fought between 58 and 51 B.C. Keep in mind that B.C. dates run "backwards"; for example, 58 B.C. came seven years before 51 B.C. This choice does not list the battles in proper order.

· ·

Answer: a. The only conclusion that it is fair to draw from the map is that the Romans conquered Aquitania and Belgica.

· ·

Answer: c. The map shows that the Loire and Garonne rivers both flow into the Atlantic Ocean.

Use the graphic to answer the following two questions.

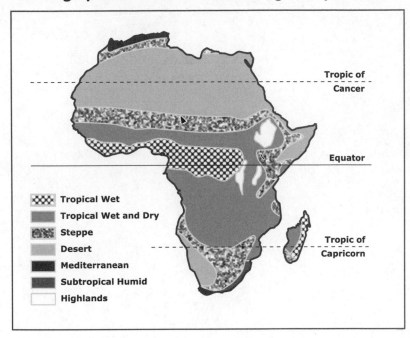

Legend:
- Tropical Wet
- Tropical Wet and Dry
- Steppe
- Desert
- Mediterranean
- Subtropical Humid
- Highlands

Map labels: Tropic of Cancer, Equator, Tropic of Capricorn

According to the map, what is the primary climate of the northern third of Africa?

a. tropical wet
b. steppe
c. subtropical humid
d. desert

· ·

It can be inferred from the map that the Mediterranean Sea borders

a. the west coast of Africa.
b. the southern tip of Africa.
c. the southeastern coast of Africa.
d. the northern coast of Africa.

· ·

———————

Answer: d. The northern third of Africa appears at the top of the map of Africa. It is made up primarily of desert; more specifically, the Sahara Desert.

. . . .

Answer: d. The northern tip of the African continent has a Mediterranean climate. No other part of the continent has such a climate. Therefore, it is reasonable to conclude that the northern coast of the African continent borders the Mediterranean Sea.

. . . .

Use the photograph and map to answer the following two questions.

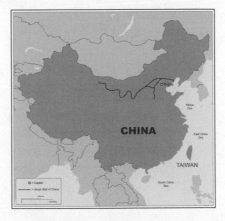

The photograph and map depict the Great Wall of China, built during the late 1400s and early 1500s.

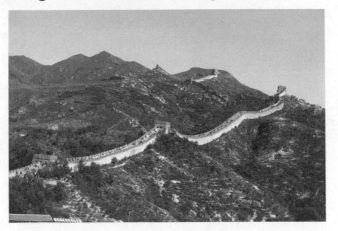

What is the approximate total length of all segments of the Great Wall of China?
a. 600 miles
b. 1,000 miles
c. 3,000 miles
d. 6,000 miles

Answer: c. Use the scale to approximate the length of the Great Wall as shown on the map to determine a total length of 3,000 miles.

For what purpose was the Great Wall of China most likely built?

a. to provide protection from military invaders from the north

b. to provide protection from military invaders from the south

c. to create a tourist attraction that would bring international travelers to China

d. to protect Beijing from flooding rivers

. . . .

Read the passage and answer the following two questions.

The Aztec empire of the thirteenth and fourteenth centuries was based on an agricultural economy. The Valley of Mexico—a fertile basin with five lakes in its center—provided land for farming. However, as the population of the empire grew, the Aztecs needed to make more land suitable for agriculture. To do this, they developed irrigation (a system that carries water through dams and canals to use for farming) and formed terraces (a process that cuts "steps" into hillsides to make flat surfaces for farming). They also practiced land reclamation, turning swamps and wet areas into land that can be cultivated.

_____

What factor caused the Aztecs to develop agricultural innovations?

a. The empire shifted from an agriculture-based economy to an industrial one.

b. Annual flooding created rich soil, but the lakes could not sustain crops the rest of the year.

c. An increase in population created a need for land for more housing.

d. A growing population resulted in increased food demands.

. . . .

Answer: a. The most likely explanation for building the Great Wall was to provide protection. The photograph shows that the wall was tall and sturdy and would thus have presented a formidable obstacle to an invading army. Because the Great Wall is built along the northern portion of China (with the city of Beijing to the south of the wall), it is most likely that the wall was built to stop invaders from the north.

Answer: d. The Aztecs needed more land for farming to produce enough food for the growing population.

GED® TEST SOCIAL STUDIES FLASH REVIEW

An island in Southern Indonesia, Bali has a hot and humid climate and volcanic soil that is good for farming rice, but much of the island is hilly. To solve this problem, Balinese rice farmers use which of the techniques also employed by the Aztecs?
a. land reclamation
b. land terracing
c. irrigation
d. landfill

. . . .

All of the following might explain the change in India's population from 1950 to 2000 EXCEPT
a. advances in healthcare.
b. improvements to national sanitation services.
c. a dramatic increase in per capita income.
d. a series of severe weather events, such as earthquakes and hurricanes.

. . . .

Answer: b. Terracing solves the problem because it creates flat surfaces out of hillsides for farming.

· ·

Answer: d. The population of India began a rapid increase in 1950 that continued through 2000. Choice d describes events that would reduce the population; each of the incorrect choices describes conditions that would promote population growth.

· ·

Use the map and paragraph to answer the following three questions.

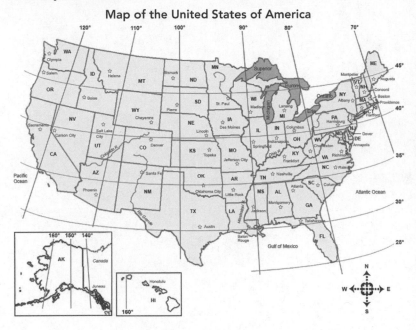

Map of the United States of America

Determining Location

Absolute location and relative location are important in determining where a specific place is located. The term *absolute location* refers to the exact location of a place. To determine absolute location, it is necessary to note lines of latitude and longitude. This is accomplished by first noting which line of latitude runs nearest the location and then noting which line of longitude runs nearest the location. The term *relative location* refers to a place's location in relation to another place. For example, Ohio is located to the northwest of Louisiana. Indiana is located at the most southern point of Lake Michigan.

———————————

The *relative location* of Austin, Texas can be described as

a. 30.25° N, 97.75° W.

b. east of the most western point of the Rio Grande River.

c. 33.75° N, 84.39° W.

d. west of the most eastern point of Sacramento, California.

· ·

Answer: b. Austin's relative location can be described as being to the east of the most western point of the Rio Grande River.

Fill in the blank with either *absolute location* or *relative location.*

Maria is discussing directions to her office with a business client who has just arrived from a nearby city. Since the client's last visit, Maria's office has relocated to a location several miles away from the former office location. Maria's client will be driving to the new location. The term that identifies the most effective type of location Maria should be discussing with the client is

_____.

. . . .

Which city is located nearest 35° N, 105° W?
a. Atlanta
b. Des Moines
c. Jefferson City
d. Santa Fe

. . . .

Answer: relative location. The paragraph provides terms that describe location: "The term *relative location* refers to a place's location in relation to another place." Absolute location provides latitude and longitude, which would not be the most effective way to communicate the location to the client, who will be driving to Maria's office.

· ·

Answer: d. Locating the specified lines of latitude and longitude leads to Santa Fe, New Mexico.

· ·

Use the pie chart to answer the following two questions.

President's Proposed Federal Budget, 2008

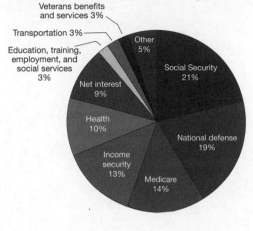

Which of the following statements is a FACT found in the pie chart?
a. The United States spends too much on Social Security.
b. National defense is the single largest expense in the federal budget.
c. The federal government spends more on health than it spends on education.
d. Increased spending on public transportation would benefit the environment.

· ·

Answer: c. The pie chart shows that the government spends 10% of its budget on health and 3% of its budget on education.

· ·

The data in the pie chart does NOT support which of the following conclusions?
a. "Other" expenses include spending on interest on the national debt.
b. Transportation constitutes a relatively small portion of the federal budget.
c. National defense is an important priority for the federal government.
d. The federal government spends more on income security than it spends on net interest.

. . . .

"You shall not deduct interest from loans to your countryman, whether in money or food or anything else that can be deducted as interest."
—*Deuteronomy*, 23:20

"That which you seek to increase by interest will not be blessed by God; but the alms you give for his sake shall be repaid to you many times over."
—Koran

"If indeed someone has fallen into the error of presuming to stubbornly insist that the practice of interest is not sinful, we decree that he is to be punished as a heretic."
—Canon 29 of the Roman Catholic Council of Vienne (1311), 30:39

What is the best conclusion that can be drawn from the three quotations?
a. Judeo-Christian law is the basis of modern economic theory.
b. Many religious precepts are at odds with banking.
c. Money lending was an honored position in medieval Europe.
d. The Catholic Church reversed its ban on usury.

. . . .

Answer: a. The pie chart includes a section for Net Interest. That is the portion of the budget dedicated to paying interest on the national debt.

• •

Answer: b. All three quotations condemn the practice of charging interest, which is at the heart of modern banking and economics.

• •

Use the information to answer the following two questions.

The law of supply and demand is a basic economic principle. Demand refers to how much of a product or service is desired by consumers at a certain price. Supply refers to the quantity producers are willing to provide at a certain price. The point at which the supply and demand curves meet dictates the price. This is sometimes called the equilibrium.

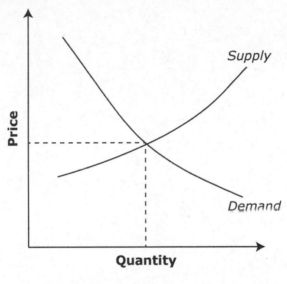

What can you conclude from this information?
a. Supply stays the same regardless of the price.
b. When the price is higher, supply will be lower.
c. Demand stays the same regardless of the price.
d. When the price is higher, demand will be lower.

_____

Answer: d. When a product costs more, fewer people will want to buy it.

In this excerpt, a *producer* refers to:
a. a seller of a product or service
b. a buyer of a product or service
c. a creator of a movie or recording
d. a person or company that decides the price of a product

· ·

The following chart reveals the demand for pizza at a local restaurant. What is the best generalization based on the data in the chart?

Demand for Pizza

Price	Number of slices of pizza sold
$3.00	6
$2.50	18
$2.00	30
$1.50	45
$1.00	66

a. Advertising has no effect on the price of an object.
b. The highest profit can be made by selling pizza at $2.00 a slice.
c. Price has little effect on the demand for an object.
d. Demand for an object rises as the price falls.

· ·

Answer: a. Producers include the manufacturers and the sellers of a product.

. . . .

Answer: d. The chart reveals that more people buy slices of pizza when the price declines.

. . . .

Use the information below to answer the following question.

U.S. Consumer Price Index (CPI)
Urban Consumers—
U.S. City Average—All Items

Year	CPI (Annual Average)
1966	32.4
1971	40.5
1976	56.9
1981	90.9
1986	109.6
1991	136.2
1996	156.9
2001	177.1
2006	201.6
2011	218.0

The consumer price index (CPI) is an indicator of the general level of prices. It measures the average change of prices over time. The CPI consists of a set market basket of typical goods and services such as energy, food, housing, clothes, transportation, medical care, and entertainment. When the CPI goes down, consumers have to pay less for the same amount of goods and services. The CPI for all urban consumers covers about 80 percent of the total population.

_____

Based on the data in the chart, what is the most likely prediction for 2016?
a. The U.S. trade deficit will worsen.
b. Inflation will continue.
c. Unemployment will rise.
d. Americans will be able to afford more goods.

· ·

GED® TEST SOCIAL STUDIES FLASH REVIEW

———————

Answer: b. CPI is a measure of inflation, and it has been rising consistently for the past 50 years.

· ·

Use the information below to answer the following two questions.

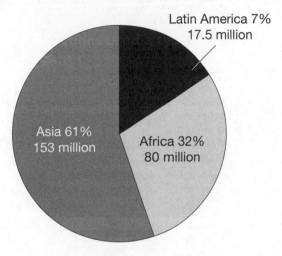

The World's Child Laborers

Of the world's 250 million child laborers, 186 million are under age five, and 170 million perform hazardous work. Most working children in rural areas labor in agriculture, while urban children work in trade and services, with a smaller percentage working in manufacturing, construction, and domestic service.

Source: Data from the International Labor Organization (ILO), www.ilo.org.

Based on the graph and passage, where would child-labor reform measures be the most effective?
a. in Europe
b. in rural areas
c. in the developing world
d. in areas where children are employed to work in mines

Answer: c. The majority of child labor takes place in the developing world, of which Africa, Asia, and Latin America are a part. You can theorize that the most effective reform measures would target the areas where most working children live.

. . . .

Which conclusion can be made using the details provided in the chart?
a. Eighty million African children work.
b. Child labor is a worldwide problem.
c. The problem of child labor has grown substantially in recent decades.
d. If children work, they are most likely not attending school.

. . . .

Answer: b. Choice b is the only valid conclusion that can be made based on the chart.

· ·

Use the chart to answer the following question.

Ten Fastest Growing Occupations, 2000–2010			
Occupation	Projected Growth %	Income Rank	Education and Training
Computer software engineers, applications	100	1	Bachelor's degree
Computer support specialists	97	2	Associate's degree
Computer software engineers, systems software	90	1	Bachelor's degree
Network and computer systems administrators	82	1	Bachelor's degree
Network systems and data communications analysts	77	1	Bachelor's degree
Desktop publishers	67	2	Post-secondary vocational certificate
Database administrators	66	1	Bachelor's degree
Personal and home care aides	62	4	Short-term on-the-job training
Computer systems analysts	60	1	Bachelor's degree
Medical assistants	57	3	Moderate on-the-job training
Income rank categories 1 = very high ($39,700 and over) 2 = high ($25,760 to $39,660) 3 = low ($18,500 to $25,760) 4 = very low (up to $18,490)			

Source: U.S. Department of Labor, Bureau of Labor Statistics.

Which of the following statements is supported by the information presented?

a. The largest number of jobs in the United States will be computer-related in the decade 2000–2010.

b. Computer-related jobs are the best paying in the nation.

c. Of the ten fastest growing jobs, the lowest paying is medical assistant.

d. Of the ten fastest growing jobs, the best paying require the most education.

GED® TEST SOCIAL STUDIES FLASH REVIEW

Answer: d. Choice d is the only one supported by the details of the chart. Although the chart offers the rate of growth of occupations, it does not give the overall number of jobs available.

What is the best conclusion based on the two pie graphs?

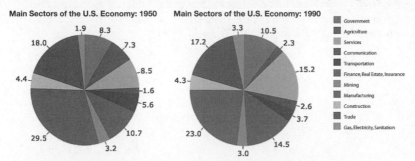

Main Sectors of the U.S. Economy: 1950

Main Sectors of the U.S. Economy: 1990

Government
Agriculture
Services
Communication
Transportation
Finance, Real Estate, Insurance
Mining
Manufacturing
Construction
Trade
Gas, Electricity, Sanitation

a. The service industry became more important to the U.S. economy toward the end of the twentieth century.
b. The U.S. economy shrank under Republican presidents.
c. The construction industry followed the housing boom toward the end of the twentieth century.
d. The U.S. economy stagnated between 1950 and 1990.

. . . .

Which conclusion can most fairly be drawn from this chart?

United Auto Workers (UAW) Membership

Year	Number of Members
1970	1,619,000
1980	1,446,000
1990	952,000
2000	672,000
2010	377,000

(Membership numbers rounded to the nearest thousand)

a. The UAW has failed to help its members.
b. There has been a decline in the number of automobiles on American roads.
c. Automobile manufacturing has declined in the United States.
d. U.S. labor laws have made it more difficult for workers to join a union.

. . . .

Answer: a. Use the process of elimination. A service economy consists of those economic sectors not involved in the production or processing of goods and energy. In the United States, service and finance sectors increased from 19.2% in 1950 to 29.7% in 1990.

. . . .

Answer: c. Automobile manufacturing has moved from the United States to other countries in recent decades, contributing to a decline in the number of U.S. auto workers.

. . . .

The subjects of every state ought to contribute towards the support of the government, as nearly as possible, in proportion to their respective abilities; that is, in proportion to the revenue which they respectively enjoy under the protection of the state. The expense of government to the individuals of a great nation is like the expense of management to the joint tenants of a great estate, who are all obliged to contribute in proportion to their respective interests in the estate.

—Adam Smith, *The Wealth of Nations*, Book V, Chapter 2

_____

Based on this quotation, Adam Smith would most likely support which of the following?
a. anti-trust legislation
b. a flat tax
c. a graduated income tax
d. parliamentary government

. . . .

Use the passage below to answer the following two questions.

Laissez-faire economics refers to the idea that people are most productive when governments leave them alone to do whatever they please. The term was coined by the Physiocrats, a group of eighteenth-century French thinkers. The Physiocrats believed that the government should do nothing to hinder free competition among producers and sellers. They also thought that there should be no restrictions on foreign trade, and that countries that practiced free trade would grow rich. However, other economists, called Mercantilists, believed just the opposite. The Mercantilists thought that the government should try to control foreign trade to make it more profitable. Of course, neither the Physiocrats nor the Mercantilists ever imagined today's world of multinational corporations. Today, *laissez-faire* can sometimes mean leaving corporations free to form unfair monopolies. Nevertheless, free trade remains popular in major exporting countries such as the United States.

_____

What is the author's attitude toward *laissez-faire* economics?
a. It is the most useful economic policy ever invented.
b. It was wrong from the start.
c. It should immediately be applied in the United States.
d. It is not always the best policy in today's world.

. . . .

Answer: c. In the selection, Adam Smith supports "taxes in proportion to the revenue which they respectively enjoy. . . ."

. . . .

Answer: d. The last two sentences in the passage suggest that *laissez-faire* economics can lead to problems such as unfair monopolies that hinder competition.

. . . .

How did the Physiocrats differ from the Mercantilists?
a. The Mercantilists favored farming; the Physiocrats favored industry.
b. The Physiocrats favored government regulation; the Mercantilists did not.
c. The Physiocrats favored the wealthy; the Mercantilists favored the poor.
d. The Mercantilists favored government regulation; the Physiocrats did not.

. . . .

Use the passage to answer the following two questions.

A **standard of living** is essentially the minimum of the necessities or luxuries of life to which a person or a group is accustomed. The average standard of living in a country may be measured by first determining the country's gross national product, or GNP (the value of the goods and services produced in the national economy in a given year), and then by calculating per capita GNP (the GNP divided by the number of people in the country). Per capita GNP tells how much each person would receive if all the goods and services produced in the country during the year were divided equally.

An individual's standard of living, of course, may improve or decline depending on circumstances. Retirement from employment, for instance, often leads to a decline in the standard of living as retirees attempt to live on a percentage of their former income. The average standard of living in a country may be subject to change due to political upheaval, forces of nature, or global economics.

Which of these circumstances would almost certainly improve a person's standard of living?
a. divorcing a spouse
b. having a child
c. receiving a college diploma
d. filing tax forms on time

. . . .

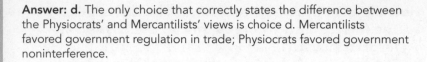

Answer: d. The only choice that correctly states the difference between the Physiocrats' and Mercantilists' views is choice d. Mercantilists favored government regulation in trade; Physiocrats favored government noninterference.

· ·

———————

Answer: c. The passage says that an individual's standard of living may improve or decline depending on personal circumstances, such as retirement. However, divorcing a spouse is no guarantee of improvement; in fact, many divorced people experience a decline in living standards.

· ·

Country X has a larger gross national product than Country Y. To find out whether the standard of living is higher in Country X, what else would you need to know?
a. the number of school-age children in Countries X and Y
b. the size of the populations of Countries X and Y
c. the number of retirees in Countries X and Y
d. the number of unemployed workers in Countries X and Y

. . . .

Answer: b. According to the passage, the average standard of living in a country may be measured by first determining the country's gross national product (GNP) and then by calculating per capita GNP. The way to calculate per capita GNP is to divide the GNP by the number of people in the country. So to compare the standards of living in Country X and Country Y, you would need to know the GNP of each country and also the number of people in each country so that you could calculate and compare per capita GNP.

• •

Use the information below to answer the following question.

Euro Conversion Rates

On January 1, 1999, 11 European countries began phasing in the "euro" to replace their national currencies. The following table shows a value of one euro in each of the 11 countries' currencies.

1 euro =

13.76	Austrian schillings
40.34	Belgian francs
2.20	Dutch guilders
5.95	Finnish markkas
6.56	French francs
1.96	German marks
0.79	Irish punts
1,936.27	Italian lire
40.34	Luxembourg francs
200.48	Portuguese escudos
166.39	Spanish pesetas

Which conclusion is best supported by the information in the table?

a. **A German mark is worth less than a Finnish markka.**

b. **An Irish punt is the currency with the greatest value of the euro.**

c. **Belgium and Luxembourg share a government.**

d. **It takes more than 200 euros to equal one Portuguese escudo.**

_____

Answer: b. One euro is worth about 4/5 of an Irish punt.

GED® TEST SOCIAL STUDIES FLASH REVIEW

Please use the graphic to answer the following question.

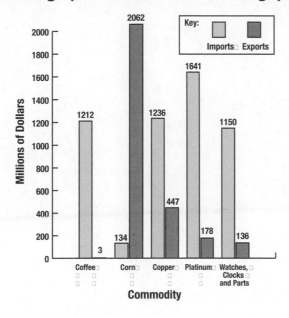

According to the graphic, which of the following items, if found in a store in the United States, would most likely be entirely American made?
a. copper tubing
b. a platinum wedding band
c. a package of frozen corn
d. a can of coffee

Answer: c. The graphic shows that the United States imports large quantities of coffee, copper, platinum, and watches and clocks. It also shows that the United States exports only very small amounts of these same commodities. These two facts suggest that the United States does not produce large amounts of these particular items. The United States exports a great deal of corn, however, and imports very little; therefore, it is reasonable to conclude that the United States produces most of the corn available on its domestic market. And it follows that if you bought a package of frozen corn in a store in the United States, that corn would likely be American made. Therefore, choice c is the best answer. All of the other choices are incorrect based on the information in the graphic.

Please use the chart below to answer the following four questions.

Unemployment Rates in Selected Countries, 1995

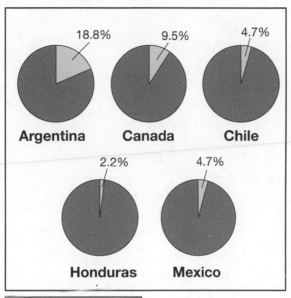

18.8%   9.5%   4.7%

Argentina   Canada   Chile

2.2%   4.7%

Honduras   Mexico

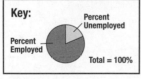

Key:

Percent Unemployed

Percent Employed

Total = 100%

What was Canada's approximate rate of unemployment in 1995?
a. 40%
b. 25%
c. 10%
d. 3%

Answer: c. In the circle graph for Canada, the shaded portion is about 10% of the whole. Therefore, unemployment was about 10%.

Which two countries had about the same unemployment rate?
a. Chile and Mexico
b. Canada and Argentina
c. Chile and Argentina
d. Argentina and Mexico

· ·

High unemployment is generally associated with a low growth rate and a low level of inflation. Based on the graphs, which country would you expect to have the lowest level of inflation?
a. Argentina
b. Chile
c. Honduras
d. Mexico

· ·

Which conclusion can you fairly draw from these data?
a. Workers travel to Chile from Mexico to earn higher wages.
b. A laborer from Honduras could easily find work in Argentina.
c. Honduras is the poorest nation in the western hemisphere.
d. Chile and Argentina, though neighbors, have different economic conditions.

Answer: a. In the circle graphs for Chile and Mexico, the shaded portions are about the same; each is about 5%.

. . . .

Answer: a. If high unemployment is associated with low inflation, then the country with the highest unemployment rate is likely to have the lowest level of inflation. Of the countries shown, Argentina has the highest unemployment rate.

. . . .

Answer: d. The circle graphs show similar unemployment rates in Chile and Mexico, so there is no reason to think that demand for workers is any higher in Chile than it is in Mexico. Thus, it is unlikely that workers from Mexico could earn higher wages in Chile.

Review the chart and answer the following two questions.

United States Foreign Trade Partners			
Country	Total Trade	Exports To United States (in millions)	Imports from United States (in millions)
Canada	407,995	178,786	229,209
Mexico	246,837	110,926	135,911
Japan	211,831	65,254	146,577
China	116,316	16,253	100,063
Germany	87,981	29,244	58,737
United Kingdom	85,038	41,579	43,459
Korea (South)	68,202	27,902	40,300

Source: U.S. Census Bureau.

Which of the following conclusions can you draw from the information in the chart?
a. The United States trades the most with the countries that are geographically closest to it.
b. Geographic location does not influence international trade.
c. There is a relationship between the size of a country and its economic status.
d. There is a relationship between the population density of a country and its economic status.

_____

Answer: a. The countries that the United States trades the most with—Canada and Mexico—are also its geographic neighbors.

· ·

Which of the following statements is best supported by the chart?
a. The level of goods and services imported to the United States has increased in the past decade.
b. Policies that restrict international trade do not have any effect on the U.S. economy.
c. Japan imports and exports more than any other country in the world.
d. The most important U.S. trade partners are industrialized, developed nations.

. . . .

Answer: d. Most of the countries listed as the United States' top trade partners are industrialized, developed nations.

· ·

Use the chart to answer the following two questions.

Year	Annual CPI	Annual Inflation Rate %
Consumer Price Index (CPI)—All Urban Consumers 1982–1984 = 100		
1920	20.0	15.6
1930	17.5	–2.3
1940	14.0	0.7
1950	24.1	1.3
1960	29.6	1.7
1970	38.8	5.7
1980	82.4	13.5
1990	130.7	5.4
2000	172.2	3.4

The Consumer Price Index (CPI) measures changes in the cost of living by comparing the prices in common goods and services like food, clothing, rent, fuel, and others. This chart uses the years 1982–1984 as a base period (1982–1984 = 100). An item that costs $100 in the base period would cost the amount listed in the CPI column for that year.

Source: U.S. Department of Labor, Bureau of Labor Statistics.

The inflation rate peaked in 1920 following World War I. What other time period was marked by a high inflation rate?
a. the years immediately following the stock market crash of 1929
b. the year following the oil crisis of 1979
c. the recession of 1990
d. the years preceding the U.S. entry into World War II

. . . .

Based on the information given, which decade experienced a decrease in the cost of living?
a. 1930–1940
b. 1940–1950
c. 1950–1960
d. 1970–1980

. . . .

_____

Answer: b. The second highest inflation rate listed on the chart is 13.5% in 1980, the year following the oil crisis of 1979.

· ·

Answer: a. The CPI decreased from 17.5 in 1930 to 14 in 1940.

· ·

The following chart depicts crude oil prices between 1970 and 2012.

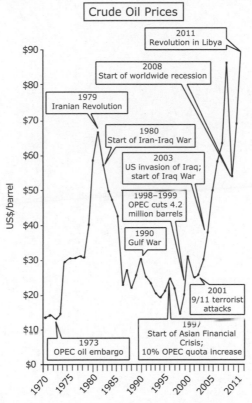

Crude Oil Prices

2011
Revolution in Libya

2008
Start of worldwide recession

1979
Iranian Revolution

1980
Start of Iran-Iraq War

2003
US invasion of Iraq;
start of Iraq War

1998–1999
OPEC cuts 4.2
million barrels

1990
Gulf War

2001
9/11 terrorist
attacks

1997
Start of Asian Financial
Crisis;
10% OPEC quota increase

1973
OPEC oil embargo

US$/barrel

Source of Data: Vehicle Technologies Office; US Department of Energy (http://www1.eere .energy.gov/vehiclesandfuels/facts/m/2012_fotw742.html); WTRG Economics (http://www.wtrg .com/oil_graphs/oilprice1970.gif).

Since 1970, the price of oil has fluctuated. According to the chart, what is the most common cause of increases in oil prices?
a. the manipulations of oil speculators
b. the control of the market by OPEC
c. conflict in the Arab World and Middle East
d. shocks to the world economy

GED® TEST SOCIAL STUDIES FLASH REVIEW

Answer: c. The graph shows that conflicts in the Arab World and Middle East are the most common causes of price increases. Rapidly rising prices all occurred during a number of these conflicts, including the Libyan Revolution.

John Maynard Keynes was an economist whose prescriptions for managing a national economy included increasing public spending and public employment during economic downturns when the private sector has cut back on its spending. President Franklin Roosevelt's New Deal included many programs that followed the advice of Keynes. One part of the New Deal that would not fall under the above Keynesian recommendation was
a. the Tennessee Valley Authority, which built hydroelectric dams along the Tennessee River.
b. the Works Progress Administration, which provided jobs to the unemployed.
c. the Social Security System, which provided pensions to millions of the elderly and the disabled.
d. the Glass-Steagall Banking Act, which separated commercial banking from investment banking.

. . . .

Monetary policy is the control of the supply of money and interest rates by the monetary authority of a country. Which of the following controls monetary policy in the United States?
a. the president
b. the Congress
c. the Supreme Court
d. the Federal Reserve

. . . .

Answer: d. The Glass-Steagall Banking Act, which separated commercial banking from investment banking, addressed an inherent conflict of interest in the banking system but did not directly increase investment during economic downturns.

· ·

Answer: d. The Federal Reserve controls monetary policy in the United States.

· ·

Which of the following is the most reasonable explanation for a shortage of a product?
a. Customers found the product overpriced.
b. The producers overestimated the demand for the product.
c. The producers underestimated the demand for the product.
d. A rival company produced a cheaper version of the product.

• •

Cyclical unemployment is job loss that is caused by a recession or by fluctuations in the economy. Which of the following is an example of cyclical unemployment?
a. construction workers in the Northeast who are out of work during cold months
b. agricultural workers who are unemployed during non-growing seasons
c. employees who quit their jobs because they are dissatisfied
d. airline employees who are laid off because slow economic times have discouraged people from traveling

• •

By 1878, the Standard Oil Company, owned by John D. Rockefeller, had bought out most of its business rivals and controlled 90% of the petroleum refineries in the United States. Which of the following was a likely effect of Standard Oil's business practices?
a. The company set limits on its prices.
b. The company increased oil prices.
c. Competition in the oil market flourished.
d. Standard Oil increased its efforts to attract needed customers.

Answer: c. If the product were overpriced, overproduced, or had few uses, there would likely be a surplus of the product rather than a shortage.

. . . .

Answer: d. Employees who are laid off because of the effects of a recession are an example of cyclical unemployment.

. . . .

Answer: b. By eliminating its competitors, Standard Oil controlled most of the production of oil and could artificially drive up prices.

Use the graph and text to answer the following question.

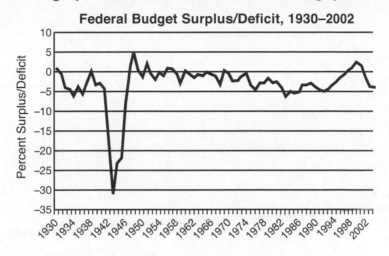

Federal Budget Surplus/Deficit, 1930–2002

Each year the federal government collects revenues in the form of taxes and other fees. It also spends money on such necessary functions as national defense, education, and healthcare. When the government collects more than it spends, it operates at a surplus. In the graph, the government operated at a surplus for every year in which the line is above 0%. When the government spends more than it collects, it operates at a deficit. In the graph, the government operated at a deficit for every year in which the line is below 0%.

_____

In what year between 1930 and 2002 did the federal government operate with the greatest budget deficit?
a. 1930
b. 1945
c. 1951
d. 1994

GED® TEST SOCIAL STUDIES FLASH REVIEW

_____

Answer: b. The graph shows that the federal government operated at approximately a 30% deficit in 1945. This is by far the largest deficit shown on the graph.

Use the chart to answer the following four questions.

Unemployment Rates in Selected Countries, 2012

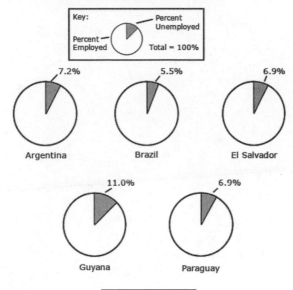

In Argentina, roughly how many people were unemployed in 2012?
a. Fewer than 1 of every 100 people
b. About 1 of every 10 people
c. About 7 of every 100 people
d. More than 7 of every 10 people

. . . .

Which two countries had roughly the same unemployment rate in 2012?
a. Argentina and Brazil
b. Brazil and El Salvador
c. Guyana and Paraguay
d. El Salvador and Paraguay

. . . .

GED® TEST SOCIAL STUDIES FLASH REVIEW

Answer: c. Argentina has an unemployment rate of 7.2%, meaning that roughly 7 of every 100 people are unemployed.

· ·

Answer: d. In the pie charts for El Salvador and Paraguay, the shaded portions are about the same.

· ·

High unemployment is generally associated with a low growth rate and a low level of inflation. Based on the graphs, which country would you expect to have the lowest level of inflation?

a. Argentina
b. Brazil
c. Guyana
d. Paraguay

. . . .

Which conclusion can you fairly draw from the data on the pie charts?

a. Guyana is the poorest nation in the Western Hemisphere.
b. Workers travel from Brazil to Paraguay to earn higher wages.
c. Unemployment is directly tied to a country's level of education.
d. The neighboring countries of Brazil and Guyana have different economic conditions

. . . .

Answer: c. Guyana has the highest level of unemployment, which is associated with low levels of inflation.

· ·

Answer: d. As shown in the pie charts, Brazil and Guyana have vastly different unemployment rates.

· ·

In 1932, while campaigning for president, Franklin D. Roosevelt said the following:

"If the Nation is living within its income, its credit is good. If, in some crises, it lives beyond its income for a year or two, it can usually borrow temporarily at reasonable rates. But if, like a spendthrift, it throws discretion to the winds, and is willing to make no sacrifice at all in spending; if it extends its taxing to the limit of the people's power to pay and continues to pile up deficits, then it is on the road to bankruptcy."

In 1981, Ronald Reagan made the following statement during his Inaugural Address:

"For decades, we have piled deficit upon deficit, mortgaging our future and our children's future for the temporary convenience of the present. To continue this long trend is to guarantee tremendous social, cultural, political, and economic upheavals."

Roosevelt was president from 1932 to 1945. Reagan was president from 1981 to 1988.

Which of the following conclusions is supported by the quotations?
a. All presidential candidates make promises they do not intend to keep.
b. If a president cares enough about federal deficits, he or she can force the government to operate on a surplus.
c. Ronald Reagan and Franklin Roosevelt pursued virtually identical agendas during their presidencies.
d. Despite their best intentions, it is often difficult for presidents to control federal deficits.

Answer: d. Both Roosevelt and Reagan promised to avoid deficit spending, yet both generated budget deficits throughout their presidencies. Thus, the quotes support the conclusion that presidents have a hard time controlling federal deficits.

Use the table and text to answer the following three questions.

Income Per Citizen, 2006		
	Per Capita Income (US Dollars)	**PPP Income (US Dollars)**
Luxembourg	80,288	69,800
Norway	64,193	42,364
Iceland	52,764	35,115
Switzerland	50,532	32,571
Ireland	48,604	40,610
Denmark	47,984	34,740
Qatar	43,110	29,000
United States	42,000	41,399
Sweden	39,694	32,200
Netherlands	38,618	32,100

Economists use several measures to calculate the income of the average citizen of each country. Data documenting each citizen's personal income is rarely available, unfortunately, so economists must estimate personal income by dividing gross domestic product (GDP)—the value of all the goods and services produced in a country—by the number of citizens. This figure gives an inaccurate picture of how citizens live, however, because it fails to take into account the cost of goods and services in a country. A second measure, called purchasing power parity (PPP), adjusts for the domestic cost of goods to provide a more accurate picture of what each citizen's money will buy him or her. For the sake of comparison, both measures are calculated in U.S. dollars. The table shows the figures for ten of the world's wealthiest nations in 2006.

———————

Which of the following would best explain the difference between per capita income and PPP income in Norway?
a. Consumer goods are extremely costly in Norway.
b. Many consumer goods are available in Norway.
c. Norway must import most of its consumer goods from Asia.
d. Services are relatively cheap in Norway.

. . . .

_____

Answer: a. According to the passage, PPP income adjusts for the cost of living in a given country. The lower the PPP is relative to per capita income, the more expensive it is to live in that country. In Norway, PPP is much lower than per capita income; therefore, it is reasonable to conclude that consumer goods are extremely costly in Norway.

Which of the following would be an effect of listing nations in descending order by PPP income rather than by per capita income?
a. Luxembourg would no longer be at the top of the list.
b. It would be more difficult to determine where citizens can buy the most goods and services with their income.
c. Countries not currently on the list would have to be included.
d. The United States would move from eighth on the list to a higher position.

. . . .

What is the most likely reason that the author finds it "unfortunate" that "data documenting each citizen's personal income is rarely available"?
a. The author believes that such data should be private and should never be available.
b. The author believes that estimates based on gross domestic product are extremely accurate.
c. The author believes that such data would demonstrate that citizens of the United States are the wealthiest in the world.
d. The data would provide a more accurate picture of personal income in each country.

. . . .

Answer: d. If the countries in the table were rearranged by PPP, the United States would move to third on the list, right behind Luxembourg and Norway.

· ·

Answer: d. The author's purpose is to measure personal income in various countries in order to compare the countries. The reason he thinks it is unfortunate that personal income data is rarely available is because such data would provide more accurate information on the subject of the table and passage.

· ·

Capital gains tax is money paid to the federal government out of profits from the sale of financial assets, like property (land or buildings) or stocks. For which of the following would you need to pay capital gains tax?
a. cigarettes
b. groceries
c. your mortgage
d. a profitable real estate sale

. . . .

Answer: d. A capital gains tax does not apply to your income, a home that you own, or goods and services. It does apply to the profit from the sale of property or other financial assets.

. . . .

Use the excerpt below, from 15 U.S. Code 1692c: Communication in Connection With Debt Collection, to answer the following three questions.

a) Communication with the consumer generally

Without the prior consent of the consumer given directly to the debt collector or the express permission of a court . . . a debt collector may not communicate with a consumer in connection with the collection of any debt—

> (1) at any unusual time or place or a time or place known or which should be known to be inconvenient to the consumer . . . a debt collector shall assume that the convenient time for communicating with a consumer is after 8 o'clock antemeridian [A.M.] and before 9 o'clock postmeridian [P.M.], local time at the consumer's location;
>
> (2) if the debt collector knows the consumer is represented by an attorney with respect to such debt . . . or
>
> (3) at the consumer's place of employment if the debt collector knows or has reason to know that the consumer's employer prohibits the consumer from receiving such communication.

(b) Communication with third parties

Except as provided in [another] section of this title, without the prior consent of the consumer given directly to the debt collector, or the express permission of a court . . . or as reasonably necessary to effectuate a . . . judicial remedy, a debt collector may not communicate, in connection with the collection of any debt, with any person other than the consumer, his attorney, a consumer reporting agency if otherwise permitted by law, the creditor, the attorney of the creditor, or the attorney of the debt collector.

(c) Ceasing communication

If a consumer notifies a debt collector in writing that the consumer refuses to pay a debt or that the consumer wishes the debt collector to cease further communication with the consumer, the debt collector shall not communicate further with the consumer with respect to such debt, except—

> (1) to advise the consumer that the debt collector's further efforts are being terminated;
>
> (2) to notify the consumer that the debt collector or creditor may invoke specified remedies which are ordinarily invoked by such debt collector or creditor; or

(3) where applicable, to notify the consumer that the debt collector or creditor intends to invoke a specified remedy.

If such notice from the consumer is made by mail, notification shall be complete upon receipt.

Based on the law, it is clear that unless notified not to make contact, a creditor is legally permitted to call a consumer at the consumer's home regarding a debt at what time?
a. 7:00 A.M. consumer's time
b. 9:00 A.M. creditor's time
c. 7:30 P.M. consumer's time
d. 9:30 P.M. creditor's time

. . . .

Pat is a consumer who has sent a certified letter to notify a creditor as follows: "Do not contact me again regarding this debt." Pat has followed all legal requirements for the notice to the creditor. After the creditor receives this letter, which of the following actions does the creditor have the legal right to take?
a. call Pat's boss to ask the boss to discuss the debt with Pat
b. send one more letter to Pat to demand payment of the debt
c. call Pat to demand payment of the debt
d. send a letter to Pat to state that the collection agency will be taking no further action

. . . .

A *third party* is someone other than the consumer or the debt collector. Information related to communication with third parties can be found in which section(s)?
a. Section a only
b. Section b only
c. Section a and Section b
d. Section b and Section c

GED® TEST SOCIAL STUDIES FLASH REVIEW

Answer: c. The excerpt states that a creditor may call a consumer after 8:00 A.M. and before 9:00 P.M., local time at the consumer's location. So, 7:00 A.M., consumer's time, would be too early, and 9:30 P.M., consumer's time, would be too late. Based on the information provided, it's not possible to know whether the creditor's time and the debtor's time are the same, so this rules out the response *9:00 A.M. creditor's time*, and while 9:30 P.M., creditor's time, could be earlier at the consumer's location, it is not possible to know this based only on the information provided in the question.

• •

Answer: d. The excerpt states that after a consumer properly notifies a creditor to demand that the creditor stop communication with the consumer, the creditor is allowed to communicate with the consumer only to advise that the creditor will cease action or to advise that the creditor will be pursuing other remedies.

• •

Answer: c. Section a references the employer, who would be a third party, and section b focuses entirely on third parties.

Use the information below, from 15 U.S. Code 1692c: Communication in Connection With Debt Collection, to answer the following two questions.

Income Requirement to Qualify for
Lower Premiums on a Marketplace Insurance Plan*

Number of People in the Household	1	2	3	4	5	6
Annual Income	$11,490–$45,960	$15,510–$62,040	$19,530–$78,120	$23,550–$94,200	$27,570–$110,280	$31,590–$126,360

*Note that requirements other than number of people in household and annual income may apply.

The data are taken from the public domain.

Income Requirement to Qualify for Lower Premiums
and Lower Out-of-Pocket Costs on a Marketplace Insurance Plan*

Number of People in the Household	1	2	3	4	5	6
Annual Income	$11,490–$28,725	$15,510–$38,775	$19,530–$48,825	$23,550–$58,875	$27,570–$68,925	$31,590–$78,975

*Note that requirements other than number of people in household and annual income may apply.

The data are taken from the public domain.

In 2010, the Affordable Care Act was signed into law in the United States. The act is often referenced as "Obamacare." Great controversy existed before the law was passed, and great controversy has continued since its passage, with Democrats generally being favor of the act and Republicans generally being opposed to it.

After a positive U.S. Supreme Court decision regarding the Affordable Care Act, Senator John Cornyn made this statement: "If Obamacare is allowed to stand—and Congress is allowed to make the purchase of government-endorsed health insurance compulsory—there will be no meaningful limit on Washington's reach into the lives of the American people."

Senate Majority Leader Harry Reid stated, "Unfortunately Republicans in Congress continue to target the rights and benefits guaranteed under this law. They'd like to give the power back to the insurance companies, the power of life and death back to the insurance companies. But our Supreme Court has spoken. The matter is settled."

For a household of three people to qualify for lower premiums and lower out-of-pocket costs on a marketplace Insurance plan, the maximum income is $_____.

· ·

Based on the tables and paragraph, which of these claims is strongly supported?
a. John Cornyn is likely a Republican.
b. People who do not own homes will likely fail to qualify for health-care coverage.
c. Harry Reid is likely a primary author of the Affordable Care Act.
d. Households without children are more likely to apply for health-care coverage than households with children.

· ·

Answer: 48,825. The question does not ask the maximum income for a household of three to qualify for lower premiums alone, which would be $78,120; rather, the questions asks the maximum income for a household of three to qualify for lower premiums and lower out-of-pocket costs, which is $48,825.

. . . .

Answer: a. The paragraph states that Republicans generally oppose the Affordable Care Act, and Cornyn's statement makes it clear that he opposes the act, so this evidence supports the claim that he is likely a Republican.

. . . .

"Every nation on the Earth that embraces market economics and the free enterprise system is pulling millions of its people out of poverty. The free enterprise system creates prosperity, not denies it."

—Marco Rubio
U.S. Senator from Florida
August 24, 2011

Based on the quote, which inference could most clearly and reasonably be drawn regarding Rubio's opinion insofar as the free enterprise system?
a. **Poverty causes the existence of the free enterprise system.**
b. **Without prosperity, poverty and the free enterprise system would be stronger.**
c. **Poverty in nations is caused by prosperity in the free enterprise system.**
d. **Without the free enterprise system, many more people would be experiencing poverty.**

Answer: d. Rubio states that the free enterprise system is pulling millions of people out of poverty, so it is reasonable to infer that he believes that without the free enterprise system, many more people would be experiencing poverty, as they would not be pulled out of poverty.

· ·

Accessed through Northwestern University Library
https://images.northwestern.edu/multiresimages/
inu:dil-ca604a87-3606-41e8-abf8-4d52e19d8768

Which statement best describes the intent of the poster?
a. motivating people to invest in bonds so that the war effort will be successful
b. influencing airlines to provide planes that will help in creating a strong defense
c. stimulating the economy through Uncle Sam's plea to buy plane tickets more often
d. encouraging Americans to move to smaller homes so that they may purchase bonds

_____

Answer: a. The purchase of bonds provides money to the government. The government could, in turn, utilize the funds to make certain that planes—an essential component of the World War II effort—were available and could be fueled, flown, and repaired.

"The United States was born in the country and moved to the city in the nineteenth century."

—Anonymous

_____

To what great movement does this quotation refer?
a. western expansion
b. colonization
c. industrialization
d. imperialism

. . . .

———————

Answer: c. The United States was indeed "born in the country" in the sense that, at its start, the nation was overwhelmingly rural. However, the nineteenth century in the United States was the time of the Industrial Revolution. During this period, factories were built in the cities, and great numbers of people left the farms and small towns to become city-dwelling factory workers. This is the movement to which the quote refers.

· ·

Please use the passage below to answer the following three questions.

The core of the Iroquois empire extended from the Hudson River to the Genesee River in present-day central New York State and from Lake Ontario to what is now the Pennsylvania–New York border. By 1700, the Iroquois had extended their territory westward, spreading some 800 miles between the Appalachians and the Mississippi River.

The power of the Iroquois began in the 1500s, when Hiawatha brought together the Five Iroquois Nations of the New York valley and formed the Iroquois League to try and keep the peace. Although the league lasted 300 years, the so-called "Great Peace" would not last. One important reason for the destruction of the peace was the fur trade.

As the French began systematic fur trading, the Algonquians became their main suppliers of beaver pelts. Meanwhile, Dutch traders created a similar pact with the Iroquois. In a short time, both Algonquian and Iroquois territories were denuded of wildlife, and a struggle for trapping grounds ensued. The Iroquois routed the Algonquians, who fled eastward to the seashore. The French turned to the Hurons to replace the Algonquians as trading partners, but the Dutch urged their Iroquois allies to break the Huron monopoly. By the mid-1600s, the Iroquois had succeeded in destroying the Huron civilization and sending the survivors west to the plains.

According to this passage, why did Hiawatha create the Iroquois League?
a. to secure a lasting peace among the Five Iroquois Nations
b. to strengthen his bargaining position in negotiations with the Dutch
c. to form a buffer against invasion by the Algonquians
d. to extend the boundaries of the Iroquois empire

_____

Answer: a. The passage says that Hiawatha brought together the Five Iroquois Nations in a league "designed to keep the peace."

Which conclusion about the fur trade is best supported by the information presented?
a. The fur trade built friendship among the tribes.
b. European traders were generous to their American Indian partners.
c. The fur trade improved the standard of living for all.
d. The fur trade was a negative influence on tribal life.

. . . .

According to this passage, why did the Iroquois make war on the Hurons?
a. They wanted the Hurons' land to use for farming.
b. They had been attacked by the Hurons' French partners.
c. They feared that the Hurons would join forces with the Algonquians.
d. They were encouraged to do so by the Dutch.

. . . .

According to the respected American historian Frederick Jackson Turner, America's western frontier finally closed in the year 1890. Which of the following facts from the 1890 census is the best evidence for Jackson's statement?
a. In 1890, 35% of Americans lived in cities.
b. In 1890, there was no longer any single large area in the West without settlers.
c. In 1890, the population of Los Angeles reached 50,000.
d. In 1890, Chicago had become the second largest city in the United States.

Answer: d. Competition for the fur trade caused war among the Iroquois, Algonquians, and Hurons, so that "the fur trade was a negative influence on tribal life" is a fair conclusion to draw from the passage.

· ·

Answer: d. According to the passage, the Dutch urged their Iroquois allies to attack the Hurons to break the Huron monopoly over the fur trade.

· ·

Answer: b. The frontier referred to the hypothetical boundary between settled areas of the United States and open territory that had not yet been settled by people. With no single area in the West without settlers in 1890, the frontier, in effect, no longer existed.

Use the photograph and passage to answer the following two questions.

After 72 years of campaigning and protest, women were granted the right to vote in 1920. Passed by Congress and ratified by 36 of the then 48 states, the Nineteenth Amendment of the U.S. Constitution states: "The right of citizens of the United States to vote shall not be denied or abridged by the United States or by any State on account of sex."

Source: National Archives and Record Administration.

Who are the women in this photograph addressing?
a. other women who say they don't want the right to vote
b. President Woodrow Wilson
c. abolitionists
d. suffragettes

. . . .

With which of the following statements would the photographer most likely agree?
a. Women should behave in a dignified and orderly manner even if they are protesting.
b. Women stand outside the gates of governmental power.
c. The suffragettes would be more effective if they had more powerful slogans.
d. Demonstrations are the most effective ways to influence lawmaking.

. . . .

Answer: b. The women in the photograph hold posters that ask, "MR. PRESIDENT HOW LONG MUST WOMEN WAIT FOR LIBERTY." Their protest is directed at President Wilson.

. . . .

Answer: b. By portraying the women picketing outside the tall gates of the White House, the photographer is making a visual statement that concurs with choice b.

. . . .

Use the map to answer the following two questions.

Allied Powers
Central Powers
Neutral Nations

The United States maintained its neutrality in the war until Germany announced its intention to use unrestricted submarine warfare in the seas. The U.S. Congress declared war on Germany on April 6, 1917. By doing so, with what other nations was it siding?
a. Bulgaria and Turkey
b. Greece and Sweden
c. Denmark and Sweden
d. Russia and Italy

Answer: d. By declaring war on Germany, the United States joined forces against the Central Powers and thus with the Allied Powers, which included Russia and Italy.

· ·

U.S. President Woodrow Wilson called the war one "to make the world safe for democracy." Based on the map and this quotation, what conclusion can be drawn?
a. **Communist Russia was a threat to democracy in 1917.**
b. **In 1917, Italy had become a fascist state that threatened democracy.**
c. **Spain did not have a representative government in 1917.**
d. **Germany and Austria-Hungary were not democracies in 1917.**

. . . .

Read the passage and answer the following three questions.

In January 1863, during the Civil War, President Abraham Lincoln's *Emancipation Proclamation* freed more than three million slaves who lived in the Confederate states. Lincoln stated: "And by virtue of the power and for the purpose aforesaid, I do order and declare that all persons held as slaves within said designated states and parts of states are, and henceforward shall be, free; and that the Executive Government of the United States, including the military and naval authorities thereof, will recognize and maintain the freedom of said persons. And I hereby enjoin upon the people so declared to be free and abstain from all violence, unless in necessary self-defense; and I recommend to them that, in all cases when allowed, they labor faithfully for reasonable wages. And I further declare and make known that such persons, of suitable condition, will be received into the armed service of the United States to garrison forts, positions, stations, and other places, and to man vessels of all sorts in said service."

Source: HistoryCentral.com.

_____

According to the passage, which of the following was NOT one of Lincoln's expectations for the former slaves?
a. **to fight for the Union army**
b. **to become free citizens**
c. **to join the paid workforce**
d. **to incite a rebellion among slaves in states that were loyal to the Union**

. . . .

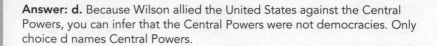

Answer: d. Because Wilson allied the United States against the Central Powers, you can infer that the Central Powers were not democracies. Only choice d names Central Powers.

· ·

————————

Answer: d. Lincoln stated that freed slaves should "abstain (withhold) from all violence, unless in necessary self-defense." He most likely did not want freed slaves to begin rebellions in areas where states loyal to the Union still held slaves.

· ·

Based on the values expressed in the *Emancipation Proclamation*, which of the following groups would have DISAPPROVED of it?
a. nations like Great Britain and France where there was strong anti-slavery sentiment
b. Confederate leaders
c. abolitionists
d. Union armed forces

. . . .

Which of the following is the most likely reason that Lincoln did not emancipate all slaves?
a. Lincoln did not want to appease radical abolitionist groups.
b. He believed slavery was an economic necessity.
c. He did not want to upset the slaveholding states that were loyal to the Union—Delaware, Maryland, Kentucky, and Missouri.
d. Lincoln did not believe that the complete abolition of slavery was possible.

. . . .

Answer: b. The basic value expressed by the proclamation is liberty for enslaved people. Although it had limitations—it freed only slaves in states that had seceded—the proclamation marked a shift in Lincoln's policy. Slavery was completely abolished in 1865 with the Thirteenth Amendment. Pro-slavery Confederate leaders had the most reason to dislike the proclamation. They feared it would cause rebellion.

· ·

Answer: c. Lincoln was reluctant to issue an order that abolished slavery throughout the nation out of loyalty to the four slaveholding border states that stayed with the Union.

· ·

Use the map to answer the following four questions.

Time Zones across the Continental United States

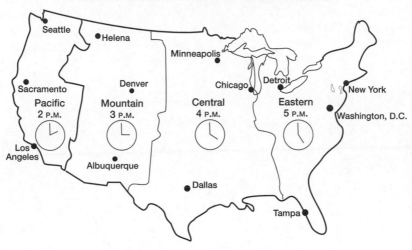

The Earth is divided into 24 time zones. The Earth rotates 15 degrees in one hour, so each time zone equals 15 degrees of longitude. The map illustrates the four time zones across the continental United States.

According to the map, what time is it in Dallas when it is noon in Sacramento?
a. 2:00 P.M.
b. 3:00 P.M.
c. 2:00 A.M.
d. 1:00 A.M.

. . . .

What time is it in Sacramento, California, when it is midnight in Tampa, Florida?
a. 1:00 A.M.
b. 12:00 P.M.
c. 9:00 A.M.
d. 9:00 P.M.

. . . .

Answer: a. Dallas falls in the Central time zone, which is two hours ahead of Sacramento, located in the Pacific time zone.

. . . .

Answer: d. Sacramento falls in the Pacific time zone, which is three hours behind Tampa, located in the Eastern time zone.

. . . .

As a traveler moves west, she can expect to
a. change time zones.
b. move into an earlier time zone for every 15 degrees of latitude she travels.
c. experience jet lag.
d. move into an earlier time zone for every 15 degrees of longitude she travels.

. . . .

In presidential elections, polling places typically close at 8 P.M. local time. In past elections, television networks have made predictions about which candidate is likely to win as soon as polls closed on the East Coast.

Which of the following statements explains why this would anger some voters?
a. The polls close later in New York than in Chicago.
b. Voters in the Central time zone want to know who won in the eastern states before they cast their ballots.
c. Polls in the Pacific time zone should open earlier if voters want their votes to matter.
d. Predictions based on voting in the Eastern time zone may influence those who have not yet voted in the Pacific time zone.

. . . .

Answer: d. As illustrated on the map, a traveler would enter an earlier time zone as he or she moves west. According to the caption, each time zone "equals 15 degrees of longitude."

· ·

Answer: d. Some voters in the Pacific time zone have not yet cast their votes when the polls close in the east. Critics feel that early predictions can affect elections in this time zone.

· ·

Read the passage and answer the following question.

The First Amendment to the U.S.Constitution states the following: "Congress shall make no law respecting an establishment of religion, or prohibiting the free exercise thereof; or abridging the freedom of speech, or of the press; or the right of the people peaceably to assemble, and to petition the Government for a redress of grievances."

———————

Which of the following situations is NOT protected by the First Amendment?

a. A *New York Times* editorial criticizes the government's foreign policy.

b. A neo-Nazi group applies for a permit and stages a rally in a public square.

c. A criminal threatens to kill his victim if the victim does not forfeit his wallet.

d. A group meets in a chapel to worship.

Answer: c. The First Amendment protects political and religious speech. It does not give someone the right to threaten another person.

. . . .

Read the excerpt below and answer the following two questions.

Beginning in 1958 . . . local NAACP [National Association for the Advancement of Colored People] chapters organized sit-ins, where African Americans, many of whom were college students, took seats and demanded service at segregated all-white lunch counters. It was, however, the sit-in demonstrations at Woolworth's store in Greensboro, North Carolina, beginning on February 1, 1960, that caught national attention and sparked other sit-ins and demonstrations in the South. One of the four students in the first Greensboro sit-in, Joe McNeil, later recounted his experience: ". . . we sat at a lunch counter where blacks never sat before. And people started to look at us. The help, many of whom were black, looked at us in disbelief too. They were concerned about our safety. We asked for service, and we were denied, and we expected to be denied. We asked why we couldn't be served, and obviously we weren't given a reasonable answer and it was our intent to sit there until they decided to serve us."

Source: www.congresslink.org and Henry Hampton and Steve Fayer (eds.), Voices of Freedom: *An Oral History of the Civil Rights Movement from the 1950s through the 1980s. Vintage Paperback, 1995.*

The writer has not directly stated, but would support, which of the following statements?
a. **Without the sit-in in Greensboro, NC, the civil rights movement would never have started.**
b. **Woolworth's served affordable lunches.**
c. **Local NAACP chapters were causing trouble and upsetting citizens.**
d. **The college students showed courage when they participated in the Greensboro sit-in.**

Answer: d. Although the author does not state that the college students were brave, the firsthand account notes that the African-American Woolworth's employees "were concerned" about the students' safety. This implies that the students could not be sure of what consequences they would face.

What is the author's purpose in including Joe McNeil's quotation?
a. to show that young people are the most likely to push for societal change
b. to demonstrate that everyone has a different point of view
c. to give a firsthand account of what has become a historic event
d. to discount the importance of the civil rights movement

. . . .

Answer: c. The author uses Joe McNeil's account to give a first-hand description of what it was like to be a part of a significant event in the civil rights movement.

· ·

Use the engraving below to answer the following two questions.

Paul Revere made and sold this engraving depicting the "Boston Massacre," a pre-Revolutionary encounter between British troops and American colonists, in which five colonists were killed.

Source: HistoryCentral.com.

Which of the following messages did Paul Revere most likely want to convey in his engraving?
a. American colonists should not protest the presence of British troops in Boston.
b. The British troops were defending themselves against rowdy gangs of colonists.
c. British troops savagely killed unarmed citizens.
d. Americans should willingly pay the British taxes on imports of glass, paper, paint, and tea.

Answer: c. By depicting the British troops firing into an unprotected crowd, Revere most likely wanted to show them as savage killers.

What can you infer was Revere's purpose in creating and selling the engraving?
a. to make a large profit for himself
b. to calm the rebellious spirit of Boston citizens
c. to create support for the British empire
d. to fuel the revolutionary cause

. . . .

Answer: d. Revere most likely made and distributed this powerful image to further incite American colonists against the British.

· ·

Use the campaign poster and paragraph to answer the following three questions.

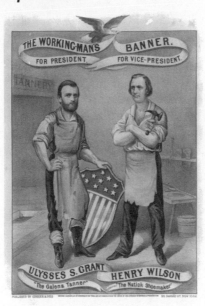

In 1872, Ulysses S. Grant ran for the presidency as the incumbent. Grant was the leader of the Radical Republicans, a faction of the Republican Party that felt the South should continue to be punished for its rebellion during the Civil War. His opponent, Horace Greeley, was also a Republican. Greeley believed that the South had suffered enough for the war and that Congress should end Reconstruction, a program under which federal troops occupied the South. Greeley formed the Liberal Republican Party; the Democratic Party also adopted Greeley as its candidate. Greeley's campaign attempted to paint the first Grant administration as deeply corrupt; this strategy failed with voters, and Grant won the election of 1872 in a landslide.

The campaign poster suggests that voters in 1872 were most concerned about
a. the corruption of the first Grant administration.
b. Grant's record as a Civil War hero.
c. whether Reconstruction should continue.
d. which candidates could best relate to their concerns.

GED® TEST SOCIAL STUDIES FLASH REVIEW

_____

Answer: d. This campaign poster portrays Grant and Wilson as working people. The subtext of the poster is that Grant and Wilson understand the common American and will represent his or her interests. It also implies that Grant's opponent, Greeley, does not understand the common American, because a campaign poster tries to persuade voters to choose one candidate over another based on the candidate's perceived advantage in a particular area.

Greeley's campaign accused Grant of corruption. Based on the campaign poster, how did Grant respond to these accusations?

a. He accused Greeley of making dishonest accusations.
b. He argued that he could not be corrupt because he had once been a tanner.
c. He chose not to address the accusations.
d. He refuted Greeley's accusation point by point.

. . . .

People who voted for Grant in 1872 almost certainly expected that a Grant victory would have which of the following results?

a. Reconstruction would continue.
b. Grant and Wilson would rebuild the White House.
c. Horace Greeley would be offered a position in the Grant administration.
d. The Radical Republicans and Liberal Republicans would split permanently.

. . . .

Answer: c. The poster does not address the issue of corruption, suggesting that Grant's strategy for dealing with the accusations was to ignore them.

· ·

Answer: a. Grant was the candidate of the Radical Republicans, a faction of the Republican Party that supported the continuation of Reconstruction. Thus, voters who chose Grant in 1872 would have expected Reconstruction to continue into his second term.

· ·

Use the photograph and quote to answer the following question.

"Following evacuation orders, this store was closed. The owner, a University of California graduate of Japanese descent, placed the I AM AN AMERICAN sign on the storefront after Pearl Harbor."
—Dorothea Lange, Oakland, CA, April 1942

Source: National Archives and Records Administration.

Which of the following statements would the photographer most likely support?
a. People of Japanese descent feel loyal to Japan first and the United States second.
b. The store owner felt that his rights as an American citizen were denied.
c. The security of the majority outweighs the rights of a minority.
d. Japanese Americans were not established members of the community.

Answer: b. Lange's image draws a powerful contrast between the grocery owner's proud statement "I AM AN AMERICAN" and the "SOLD" sign above. It is likely that she felt he was being "sold out" by his country and that his rights as an American citizen were denied.

Use the table to answer the following question.

Free African Americans in the North and South, 1820 to 1860			
	1820	1840	1860
United States	233,504	386,303	488,070
North	99,281 (83.9%)	170,728 (99.3%)	226,152 (100%)
South	134,223 (8.1%)	215,575 (8.0%)	261,918 (6.2%)

Percentages in parentheses represent percentage of total African American population.

The data in the table supports which of the following conclusions?

a. By 1820, there were no more slaves in the North.

b. Between 1820 and 1860, millions of freed slaves emigrated from the South to the North.

c. Prior to the Civil War, there were no free African Americans in the South.

d. Between 1820 and 1860, there were many more African Americans in the South than in the North.

_____

Answer: d. According to the table, there were more free African Americans in the South than in the North. In the South, free African Americans made up only a small portion of the total African American population; according to the table, over 90% of southern African Americans were slaves. This means that there were well over 1 million African Americans in the South between 1820 and 1860. Therefore, the table supports the conclusion that there were many more African Americans in the South than in the North between 1820 and 1860.

Read the passage and answer the following question.

When European settlers arrived on the North American continent at the end of the fifteenth century, they encountered diverse American Indian cultures—as many as 900,000 inhabitants with over 300 different languages. These people, whose ancestors crossed the land bridge from Asia in what may be considered the first North American immigration, were virtually destroyed by the subsequent immigration that created the United States. This tragedy is the direct result of treaties, written and broken by foreign governments, of warfare, and of forced assimilation.

Source: The Library of Congress, American Memory.

_____

What does the author of this passage believe?
a. The U.S. government was faithful to its treaties with American Indians.
b. American Indians made up a homogenous group.
c. The European settlers were responsible for the decimation of native people.
d. Native cultures were unsophisticated.

Answer: c. The author states that American Indians "were virtually destroyed by the subsequent immigration that created the United States." Choice c is a good paraphrase of that excerpt from the passage.

. . . .

Use the graph to answer the following two questions.

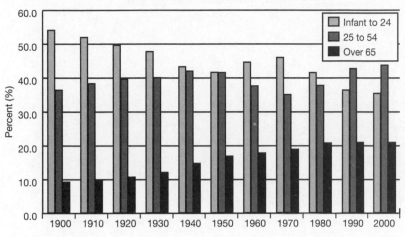

Americans by Age Group, 1900 to 2000

Which of the following conclusions is supported by the data in the graph?
a. Americans are less healthy in 2000 than they were in 1900.
b. The age of the average American has increased since 1900.
c. The average American earns more in 2000 than he or she did in 1900.
d. The number of Americans under the age of 24 has decreased since 1900.

. . . .

Answer: b. The graph provides data about Americans by age group, so it can only support conclusions about the ages of Americans.

· ·

Which of the following is an opinion based on the data in the graph?
a. About 40 percent of all Americans were between the ages of 25 and 54 in 1930.
b. In 1950, the number of Americans under the age of 25 was roughly equal to the number of Americans between the ages of 25 and 54.
c. The current trend suggests that the population of the United States is growing old too quickly.
d. More than half of all Americans were under the age of 25 in 1900.

. . . .

Read the passage and answer the following two questions.

Like so many other exploration stories, the Lewis and Clark journey was shaped by the search for navigable rivers, inspired by the quest for Edens, and driven by competition for empire. Thomas Jefferson was motivated by these aspirations when he drafted instructions for his explorers, sending them up the Missouri River in search of a passage to the Pacific. Writing to William Dunbar just a month after Lewis and Clark left Fort Mandan, Jefferson emphasized the importance of rivers in his plan for western exploration and national expansion. "We shall delineate with correctness the great arteries of this great country." River highways could take Americans into an Eden, Jefferson's vision of the West as the "Garden of the World." And those same rivers might be nature's outlines and borders for empire. "Future generations would," so the president told his friend, "fill up the canvas we begin."

Source: Library of Congress, Exhibits, "Rivers, Edens, Empires: Lewis & Clark and the Revealing of America."

————————————

Which of the following was NOT one of Jefferson's goals in sponsoring the Lewis and Clark expedition?
a. finding a waterway to the Pacific Ocean
b. mapping uncharted territory
c. setting aside vast tracts of land for native people
d. discovery of unspoiled plant and animal life

. . . .

Answer: c. Each of the incorrect choices is a fact that can be confirmed in the graph. Choice c is an opinion because it is a point that can be reasonably debated. Some people may reasonably believe that the United States is aging too quickly while others may reasonably believe that not to be the case.

Answer: c. Remember that correct answers must be supported by details from the passage. The passage never states that Jefferson had a plan for setting aside land for native people, so choice c does not describe one of Jefferson's goals in sponsoring the Lewis and Clark expedition, according to the passage.

Which historical idea best summarizes Jefferson's attitude toward the West?
a. Separation of Powers
b. Manifest Destiny
c. Pursuit of Happiness
d. Good Neighbor Policy

. . . .

Read the passage and answer the following two questions.

About the time of World War I, sharp-eyed entrepreneurs began . . . to see ways to profit from the motorist's freedom. . . . Shops could be set up almost anywhere the law allowed, and a wide variety of products and services could be counted on to sell briskly in the roadside marketplace. A certain number of cars passing by would always be in need of gas. Travelers eventually grew hungry, tired, and restless for diversions. Soon gas stations, produce booths, hot dog stands, and tourist camps sprouted up along the nation's roadsides to capitalize on these needs. As competition increased, merchants looked for new ways to snag the new market a wheel. Each sign and building had to visually shout: "Slow down, pull in, and buy." Still more businesses moved to the highway— supermarkets, motor courts, restaurants, miniature golf courses, drive-in theaters. By the early 1950s, almost anything could be bought along the roadside.

Source: Chester H. Liebs, excerpt from *Main Street to Miracle Mile.* Little, Brown and Company, 1985.

_____

What is the main idea of the passage?
a. Miniature golf was a very popular sport in the 1950s.
b. Travelers were looking for sources of entertainment.
c. Some highway businesses were more successful than others.
d. Flashy commercial enterprises sprouted along highways, eager to profit from travelers.

. . . .

Answer: b. Manifest destiny is a belief that the United States had a mandate to expand its civilization westward. Jefferson's vision of an empire with future generations filling up "the canvas we begin" most closely resembles the idea of manifest destiny.

· ·

──────────

Answer: d. Each of the incorrect choices identifies a detail from the passage. The main idea summarizes the entire passage; a detail does not.

· ·

Given the information in this passage, what appeared to be an important post–World War II trend in the United States?
a. train travel
b. car culture
c. historic preservation
d. downtown renewal

. . . .

Read the passage and answer the two questions that follow.

The Cuban Missile Crisis began in 1962 when U.S. spy planes spotted Soviet missile installations under construction in Cuba. The missiles were capable of carrying nuclear weapons and were within range of major U.S. cities. A 13-day standoff began, during which President Kennedy imposed a naval blockade of Cuba and demanded that the Soviets remove the weapons. Kennedy stated that any missile attack from Cuba would be regarded as an attack from the Soviet Union and would be responded to accordingly. Khrushchev later conceded, agreeing to remove the weapons if, in return, the United States pledged not to invade the island. Details from U.S. and Soviet declassified files and participants in the crisis have surfaced since the incident. Unknown to the U.S. government at the time, 40,000 Soviet soldiers were stationed in Cuba and armed with nuclear weapons. Although Khrushchev's actions helped to avert nuclear war, they made him appear weak to younger Soviet leaders who ousted him from power. Historians regard the crisis as the world's closest brush with the threat of nuclear war.

_____

According to the information given in this passage, it is most likely that President Kennedy
a. viewed this as a regional crisis solely between the United States and Cuba.
b. trusted Soviet officials who said there weren't any missiles in Cuba.
c. believed that the conflict was principally between the United States and the Soviet Union.
d. viewed the situation as serious but felt it could be managed with diplomacy.

. . . .

Answer: b. Roadside commercial enterprises flourished with highway construction and car travel.

· ·

———————

Answer: c. Kennedy proclaimed that any nuclear missile attack from Cuba would be regarded as an attack by the Soviet Union; thus, it is reasonable to conclude that he saw the Cuban Missile Crisis as a conflict between the United States and the Soviet Union.

· ·

Which of the following conclusions can you make based on the passage?
a. Kennedy's first concern during the crisis was the appeal of Communist ideas.
b. Nuclear war is the only way to win a cold war.
c. Kennedy knew that Khrushchev would back down.
d. The U.S. government did not know the full extent of the Soviet threat at the time.

. . . .

Answer: d. According to the passage, the United States did not know how many Soviet troops were present in Cuba. Therefore, the United States did not know the full extent of the Soviet threat at the time.

· ·

Use the illustration and text to answer the following two questions.

and Plantations in America.

JOIN, or DIE.

We hear that the General Affembly of this Province have voted

In 1754, representatives of the American colonies met to discuss their common defense and strategies for improving relations with American Indian tribes. At the meeting, Benjamin Franklin proposed closer relations among the colonies. His proposal called for a single executive and a colonial legislature to handle such matters of mutual interest as taxes, defense against the French, and American Indian relations. To promote his plan, Franklin printed the illustration in his newspaper, *The Pennsylvania Gazette*. In an accompanying editorial, he complained about "the present disunited State of the British Colonies, and the extreme Difficulty of bringing so many different Governments and Assemblies to agree in any speedy and effectual Measures for our common Defence and Security; while our Enemies have the very great Advantage of being under one Direction, with one Council, and one Purse. Hence, and from the great Distance of Britain, they presume that they may with Impunity violate the most solemn Treaties subsisting between the two Crowns . . . murder and scalp our Farmers, with their Wives and Children . . . which if they are permitted to do, must end in the Destruction of the British Interest, Trade and Plantations in America." Franklin's plan was rejected by both the King and the American colonies.

In Franklin's cartoon, the pieces of the snake represent
a. **the French army.**
b. **various American Indian tribes.**
c. **the English King and Parliament.**
d. **the British colonies.**

_____

Answer: d. The snake represents "the disunited State of the British Colonies." Note that the individual colonies are represented by letters (N.C. for North Carolina, N.J. for New Jersey, etc.).

In his editorial, Franklin makes all of the following criticisms of the system under which American colonies governed themselves EXCEPT which?

a. The system makes it impossible for the colonies to rebel against British rule.
b. The system is inefficient.
c. The system makes it difficult for the colonies to defend themselves.
d. It is too easy for the French to take advantage of weaknesses in the system.

· ·

Answer: a. Franklin never mentions rebelling against the British. This cartoon first appeared in 1754, long before there was any serious feeling among the colonists that the colonies should declare independence from Great Britain. Each of the other answers is identified in the passage.

· ·

Use the information below to answer the following two questions.

In 1972, Congress passed the Equal Rights Amendment (ERA) and put it to the states for ratification. This map shows ratification in 1979.

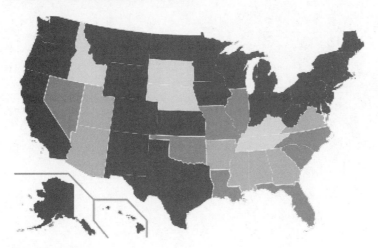

▌Ratified
▌Ratified, then rescinded
▌Not ratified, but approved by *one* house of state legislature
▌Not ratified

_____

In which region of the country did the ERA receive the least support?
a. New England
b. the Southeast
c. the Midwest
d. the Far West

_____

Answer: b. Most of the states that did not ratify the ERA are located in the Southeast.

. . . .

GED® TEST SOCIAL STUDIES FLASH REVIEW

What happened to the ERA?
a. It was passed by a majority of states and became a constitutional amendment.
b. It was no longer needed because women had made significant strides forward.
c. It did not receive the votes needed in Congress to become a constitutional amendment.
d. It did not receive the support needed by states to become a constitutional amendment.

. . . .

The cartoon below was drawn in the nineteenth century during a strike by the American Railway Union that called for a boycott of all trains with Pullman cars. Which of the following is most likely the point of view of the cartoonist?

a. Workers needed to be squeezed to get any useful work out of them.
b. The workers were being crushed by the greedy robber baron Pullman.
c. The workers needed to end their strike in order to save the train industry.
d. Pullman was a tough boss who knew how to punish lazy workers.

. . . .

Answer: d. A proposal to amend the Constitution needs to be ratified by three-quarters of the states. There are 50 states, so this means 38 states would need to ratify the amendment. As shown on the map, the ERA fell short of this number.

. . . .

Answer: b. This is the correct answer. The workers were being crushed by the greedy robber baron Pullman. In the cartoon, the employee is being attacked by Pullman, who is drawn as very fat in fancy clothes to emphasize how rich and powerful he was.

. . . .

"The accumulation of all powers, legislative, executive, and judiciary, in the same hands, whether of one, a few, or many, and whether hereditary, self-appointed, or elective, may justly be pronounced the very definition of tyranny. . . ."

—James Madison

_____

The framers of the U.S. Constitution addressed Madison's concern by incorporating which of the following into the Constitution?
a. the Bill of Rights
b. checks and balances
c. due process
d. the two-party system

. . . .

Read the excerpt from the Declaration of Independence and answer the question that follows.

"We hold these truths to be self-evident, that all men are created equal, that they are endowed by their Creator with certain inalienable rights, that among these are life, liberty, and the pursuit of happiness. . . ."

_____

What did the Founding Fathers mean by "inalienable rights"?
a. inherent rights that were given by God
b. any rights that were granted by the king
c. natural rights protected by English documents
d. the citizenship rights that Parliament had revoked

. . . .

———————

Answer: b. The system of checks and balances was intended to avoid having any one person or faction gain too much power.

· ·

———————

Answer: a. Inalienable rights, such as life, liberty, and the pursuit of happiness, cannot be taken away by anyone because they are natural rights as a human.

· ·

In 1770, outside the State House in Boston, Massachusetts, British soldiers shot and killed five colonists in an event still known as the Boston Massacre. When the soldiers were brought to trial, their lawyer was the colonist patriot John Adams. Which of the following foundational principles was most likely the key reason Adams took on this case?

a. defending the underdog
b. individual rights
c. right to bear arms
d. rule of law

. . . .

In 1734, the governor of New York, William Cosby, had the printer Peter Zenger arrested and tried for libel for accusing Cosby of corruption in the newspaper the *New York Weekly Journal*. The governor ordered copies of the newspaper burned. At the trial, the judge, who owed his job to the governor, instructed the jury that they must determine only whether the criticism was printed. They were told that it did not matter if it was true or not. The jury disagreed and found Zenger not guilty. This case was a landmark in the development of

a. governmental corruption.
b. freedom of the press.
c. book burning.
d. separation of powers.

. . . .

Answer: d. The rule of law would dictate that every accused person is entitled to a competent defense and a fair trial.

. . . .

Answer: b. The case was a landmark in the freedom of the press because the jury ignored the corrupt judges and ruled that the printer had the right to print criticism of the governor.

. . . .

In order to finance the American Revolution, the Continental Congress issued paper money that became known as Continentals. During the war, this currency was referred to by colonists in the popular phrase "worthless as a Continental," which meant that
a. they considered Continentals to be priceless.
b. they could not use Continentals as money.
c. Continentals would regain their value at the end of the war.
d. Continentals would become a sought-after collectible.

. . . .

On September 22, 1862, President Lincoln declared:

"That on the first day of January, in the year of our Lord one thousand eight hundred and sixty-three, all persons held as slaves within any State or designated part of a State, the people whereof shall then be in rebellion against the United States, shall be then, thenceforward, and forever free; and the Executive Government of the United States, including the military and naval authority thereof, will recognize and maintain the freedom of such persons, and will do no act or acts to repress such persons, or any of them, in any efforts they may make for their actual freedom."

_____

The primary motivation for the president in this statement, whose core ideas were finalized a few months later in the Emancipation Proclamation, was most likely
a. moral outrage at the dehumanization of slavery.
b. to increase the chances of the Union winning the Civil War.
c. to confirm his legacy as one of our greatest presidents.
d. the need to recruit former slaves into armed forces.

. . . .

Answer: b. They expected that they could not use Continentals as money or for anything else.

....

_____

Answer: b. Lincoln's motivation, according to most analysis, was to increase the chances of the Union winning the Civil War, since slaves would be freed only in those areas in armed rebellion.

....

At the heart of the U.S. Civil Rights Movement in the 1950s and 1960s was the use of nonviolent direct-action protest, including student sit-ins at lunch counters. Inspired by the example of Jesus, and the teachings of Mahatma Gandhi during India's struggle for independence, black church and community leaders in the United States began advocating the use of nonviolence in their own struggle. Beyond spontaneous and planned student sit-ins, several organizations were formed to fight for civil rights using Gandhi's model of nonviolent dissent and action. Three of the most influential groups—the Congress of Racial Equality (CORE), the Southern Christian Leadership Conference (SCLC), and the Student Nonviolent Coordinating Committee (SNCC)—were pivotal in bringing about social change in America.

Source: http://www.pbs.org/independentlens/februaryone/civilrights.html

---

What is the main idea of this passage?
a. **The use of nonviolent direct-action protest was at the heart of the Civil Rights Movement.**
b. **Nonviolent protest, as developed by Mahatma Gandhi, is a powerful instrument for gaining rights.**
c. **Black church and community leaders supported the use of nonviolence in the struggle for Civil Rights.**
d. **CORE, SCLC, and SNCC were civil rights organizations that provided leadership for the movement.**

. . . .

The signers of the Mayflower Compact agreed to "covenant and combine ourselves together into a civil Body Politick. . . . And by Virtue hereof do enact, constitute, and frame, such just and equal Laws, Ordinances, Acts, Constitutions, and Officers, from time to time, as shall be thought most meet and convenient for the general Good of the Colony; unto which we promise all due Submission and Obedience. . . ."

Which principal of American government was first implemented in the writing and signing of the Mayflower Compact?
a. **authority based on a written constitution**
b. **system of checks and balances**
c. **protection of individual freedoms**
d. **guarantee of equal rights for all**

. . . .

Answer: a. That the use of nonviolent direct-action protest was at the heart of the Civil Rights Movement is the main idea of the passage.

· ·

Answer: a. By signing the Compact, every adult male agreed to abide by whatever laws were made and to submit to whatever government was established based on a written constitution.

· ·

While we are now familiar with political campaigns, the first modern-style political campaign for the presidency occurred in 1840 when William Henry Harrison defeated Martin Van Buren. The campaign featured the candidate touring the country repeating his stump speech wherever he went, a smear campaign and other dirty tactics, misrepresentation of the candidates, and the first catchy campaign slogan, "Tippercanoe and Tyler, Too," which referred to Harrison's war victory over the Indian Tecumseh and to the vice presidential candidate, John Tyler. Harrison was portrayed as a man of the people while Van Buren was portrayed as an aristocrat, which was the opposite of the truth. Harrison was born into wealth while Van Buren worked his way up from humble beginnings to become vice president of the United States. The Whigs, Harrison's party, also had a great understanding of how to get out the vote and how to work the electoral college, which allocates votes to candidates based on the states they win by popular vote, to their advantage. The percentage of turnout was much higher than it is today. Even though Harrison narrowly won the popular vote, he won the electoral vote in a landslide.

According to this passage, the main cause of Harrison's victory in the 1840 presidential election was
a. lack of interest of the voters.
b. the appeal of a catchy slogan.
c. a coordinated modern campaign.
d. the lack of experience of his opponent.

· ·

Who lived in America before the Europeans arrived?

· ·

Who wrote the Declaration of Independence?

Answer: c. Taken together, all the components typical of a modern campaign were the main cause of Harrison's victory.

· ·

Answer: Native Americans lived in America before the Europeans arrived.

· ·

Answer: Thomas Jefferson

When was the Declaration of Independence adopted?

. . . .

What are the 13 original states?

. . . .

When was the Constitution written?

Answer: July 4, 1776

. . . .

Answer: Connecticut, Delaware, Georgia, Maryland, Massachusetts, New Hampshire, New Jersey, New York, North Carolina, Pennsylvania, Rhode Island, South Carolina, and Virginia.

. . . .

Answer: The Constitution was written in 1787.

What territory did the United States buy from France in 1803?

. . . .

Name one war fought by the United States in the 1800s.

. . . .

Name the U.S. war between the North and the South.

Answer: The United States bought the Louisiana Territory from France in 1803.

• •

Answer: Possible answers include the War of 1812, the Mexican-American War, the Civil War, and the Spanish-American War.

• •

Answer: The Civil War

What did the Emancipation Proclamation do?

. . . .

Who was president during the Great Depression and World War II?

. . . .

Read the passage and answer the following question.

Friends and Citizens:

The period for a new election of a citizen to administer the executive government of the United States being not far distant, and the time actually arrived when your thoughts must be employed in designating the person who is to be clothed with that important trust, it appears to me proper . . . that I should now apprise you of the resolution I have formed, to decline being considered among the number of those out of whom a choice is to be made.

———————

Based on the excerpt, when did George Washington make this speech?
a. during his tenure as general of the Continental Army
b. at the Constitutional Convention
c. prior to his first presidential nomination
d. during his second term as president

Answer: Possible answers include freed the slaves and helped preserve the Union.

. . . .

Answer: Franklin Roosevelt

. . . .

――――――――

Answer: d. Nothing in the speech says specifically where or when it occurs, so you need to look for clues—the facts or details from which you can make an inference. As you probably know, Washington was the first president. That means he did accept a nomination at some point, but at the time he is giving the speech, he does not want the nomination. So the only answer choice that makes sense by logical inference is during his second term as president.

Read the passage and answer the following two questions.

When Christopher Columbus landed in the New World, he brought with him horses, cattle, and seeds for planting. Over the next decades, European explorers and settlers brought to the New World other domesticated animals and plants. Wheat and other grains soon became staple crops in North America. Meanwhile, from the New World to the Old went corn, squash, turkeys, tomatoes, and the ever-important potato. This transfer of plants, animals, and diseases, known as the Columbian Exchange, transformed the diets and lifestyles of people on both sides of the Atlantic.

_____

Which sentence represents the main idea of the passage?
a. **When Christopher Columbus landed in the New World, he brought with him horses, cattle, and seeds for planting.**
b. **Over the next decades, European explorers and settlers brought to the New World other domesticated animals and plants.**
c. **Wheat and other grains soon became staple crops in North America. Meanwhile, from the New World to the Old went corn, squash, turkeys, tomatoes, and the ever-important potato.**
d. **This transfer of plants, animals, and diseases, known as the Columbian Exchange, transformed the diets and lifestyles of people on both sides of the Atlantic.**

. . . .

What title would best fit this passage?
a. **Trading Wheat for Corn**
b. **The Columbian Exchange**
c. **Diets on Both Sides of the Atlantic**
d. **Christopher Columbus Discovers a New World**

. . . .

Answer: d. This sentence is the main idea of the paragraph. The other sentences provide details to support this main idea.

· ·

Answer: b. All of the sentences in this paragraph lead up to the Columbian Exchange, which would be the best title for this passage.

· ·

Use the excerpt below, from the 1954 Supreme Court Decision Brown et al v. Board of Education of Topeka et al, *to answer the following four questions.*

In each of these cases, minors of the Negro race, through their legal representatives, seek the aid of the courts in obtaining admission to the public schools of their community on a non-segregated basis. In each instance, they had been denied admission to schools attended by white children under laws requiring or permitting segregation according to race. This segregation was alleged to deprive the plaintiffs of the equal protection of the laws under the Fourteenth Amendment.

[…] A three-judge federal district court denied relief to the plaintiffs on the so-called "separate but equal" doctrine announced by this court in Plessy v. Ferguson, 163 U.S.537. Under that doctrine, equality of treatment is accorded when the races are provided substantially equal facilities, even though these facilities be separate.

[…] The plaintiffs contend that segregated public schools are not "equal" and cannot be made "equal," and that hence they are deprived of the equal protection of the laws.

[…] We come then to the question presented: Does segregation of children in public schools solely on the basis of race, even though the physical facilities and other "tangible" factors may be equal, deprive the children of the minority group of equal educational opportunities? We believe that it does.

[…] Segregation of white and colored children has a detrimental effect upon the colored children. […] We conclude that in the field of public education the doctrine of "separate but equal" has no place. Separate educational facilities are inherently unequal.

> [by Chief Justice Earl Warren, writing for the majority of the Court]

According to Justice Warren, what is the question the Court must answer?
a. **Is segregation by race in public schools unfair to minority children?**
b. **Should the Court demand equal facilities in segregated schools?**
c. **Does the Court have authority over public school systems?**
d. **Does the Constitution give control of education to the states?**

Answer: a. The question the court must answer in this case, according to Justice Warren, is whether or not segregation by race in public schools is unfair to minority children.

The majority on this Court would most likely approve of which of the following?
a. creating "minorities-only" seating sections in theaters and sports arenas
b. passing laws that give majority racial groups special rights in the field of education
c. making sure that public colleges do not bar minority students on the basis of race
d. creating separate voting districts for minorities

· ·

According to the passage, the Fourteenth Amendment
a. authorizes the separation of races in public schools.
b. provides for the establishment of a nationwide public school system.
c. specifies standard nationwide voting procedures.
d. requires that people receive the equal protection of the laws.

· ·

What reason did the Court give for rejecting the doctrine of "separate but equal"?
a. Federal district courts have no power over public school systems.
b. Schools can be segregated but still have equal facilities.
c. Segregated schools are unequal by their very nature.
d. Educational achievement is difficult to measure.

Answer: c. Justice Warren, writing for the Court majority, says, "In the field of public education the doctrine of 'separate but equal' has no place." His argument is that segregation of schoolchildren by race is inherently unfair to minority children. It is logical to conclude that the Court would approve of extending this principle to public colleges by ensuring that these institutions too do not bar minority students on the basis of race.

• •

Answer: d. The passage says, "This segregation was alleged to deprive the plaintiffs of the equal protection of the laws under the Fourteenth Amendment." It is thus logical to conclude that the Fourteenth Amendment requires that people receive the equal protection of the laws.

• •

Answer: c. The Court concluded that the doctrine of "separate but equal" should be rejected because "segregation of white and colored children has a detrimental effect upon the colored children," and as a result, "separate educational facilities are inherently unequal." In other words, segregated schools are unequal (and harmful to minority children) by their very nature.

Use the chart to answer the following two questions.

U.S. presidential terms last for four years. In 1951, the Twenty-second Amendment to the U.S. Constitution became law. The amendment mandated a maximum of two four-year terms for service as U.S. President.

U.S. Presidents: Selected Presidents from 1789–1953

Name	Term of Office	Political Party
George Washington	1789–1797	Federalist
Thomas Jefferson	1801–1809	Democratic-Republican
John Quincy Adams	1825–1829	Democratic-Republican
William Henry Harrison	1841	Whig
Abraham Lincoln	1861–1865	Republican
James Abram Garfield	1881	Republican
Grover Cleveland	1885–1889; 1893–1897	Democrat
Woodrow Wilson	1913–1921	Democrat
Calvin Coolidge	1923–1929	Republican
Herbert Clark Hoover	1929–1933	Republican
Franklin Delano Roosevelt	1933–1945	Democrat
Harry S. Truman	1945–1953	Democrat

Based solely on information provided, which of the following statements can accurately be made?

a. **The end of the Federalist and Whig parties caused the creation of the Republican party.**
b. **The Whig and Democratic-Republican parties shared the same philosophy about serving the presidency and the nation.**
c. **Since the initial establishment of the U.S. presidency, equal numbers of Republicans and Democrats have served as president.**
d. **Events occurring during the Harrison and Garfield presidencies must have led to their leaving the presidency before their terms ended.**

_____

Answer: d. While it is not possible to determine exactly what the events were, it is clear that they left prior to serving an entire four-year term.

Which president's term of office would have been unconstitutional under the Twenty-second Amendment?
a. William Henry Harrison
b. James Abram Garfield
c. Grover Cleveland
d. Franklin Delano Roosevelt

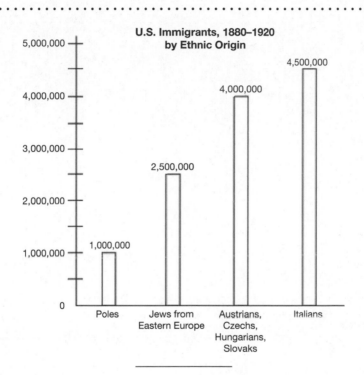

U.S. Immigrants, 1880–1920 by Ethnic Origin

Which conclusion regarding immigration to the United States is supported by information in the graph?
a. The Italians were the largest immigrant group during this period.
b. Italians and Poles immigrated because of religious persecution.
c. During this period, the population of Italy was greater than that of Poland.
d. Most immigrants during this period were Jews.

Answer: d. The paragraph explains that a presidential term is four years. The paragraph further explains that the Twenty-second Amendment mandated a maximum of two terms. Roosevelt served three full terms, and was elected to a fourth term, but died shortly after.

· ·

Answer: a. About 4.5 million Italians immigrated to the United States during that period.

· ·

Which item on the list does not fit with the others?

- **Monroe Doctrine, 1823:** The United States vows to oppose any attempt by European countries to establish colonies in Latin America or elsewhere in the Western Hemisphere.

- **Good Neighbor Policy, 1933:** The United States and Latin American countries pledge not to interfere in each other's internal affairs.

- **Marshall Plan, 1948:** The United States helps European countries to recover from the destruction of World War II.

- **Alliance for Progress, 1961:** The United States vows to help promote economic and social development in Latin America.

a. **The Good Neighbor Policy, because it involved the United States**

b. **The Monroe Doctrine, because it involves Latin America**

c. **The Alliance for Progress, because it did not have warlike aims**

d. **The Marshall Plan, because it did not involve Latin America**

Answer: d. The Marshall Plan is the only policy listed that does not deal with Latin America.

Use the passage to answer the following two questions.

We hold these truths to be self-evident, that all men are created equal, that they are endowed by their Creator with certain unalienable Rights, that among these are Life, Liberty and the pursuit of Happiness.—That to secure these rights, Governments are instituted among Men, deriving their just powers from the consent of the governed,—That whenever any Form of Government becomes destructive of these ends, it is the Right of the People to alter or to abolish it, and to institute new Government, laying its foundation on such principles and organizing its powers in such form, as to them shall seem most likely to effect their Safety and Happiness . . . when a long train of abuses . . . evinces a design to reduce them under absolute Despotism, it is their right, it is their duty, to throw off such Government, and to provide new Guards for their future security.

—excerpt from the Declaration of Independence

Which of the following is a central idea of the Declaration of Independence?
a. **Governments are stronger than the will of the people.**
b. **Governments are unnecessary if the people are virtuous.**
c. **Governments draw their legitimate power from the people.**
d. **Governments should have the unwavering support of the people.**

To gain respect for their opinions, the writers of the Declaration of Independence called on
a. **an appeal to reason.**
b. **a plea for emotional connection.**
c. **a request for partisan feeling.**
d. **a demand for religious faith.**

Answer: c. The Declaration of Independence states that "governments are instituted among men to secure inalienable rights." The last sentence makes it clear that even when a government is overthrown, a new one must be formed to "provide new Guards for their [the people's] future security."

· ·

Answer: a. The Declaration of Independence reads like a logical treatise.

· ·

Use the information below to answer the following two questions.

"[W]ould any sane nation make war on cotton? Without firing a gun, without drawing a sword, should they make war on us we could bring the whole world to our feet. . . . What would happen if no cotton was furnished for three years? I will not stop to depict what every one can imagine, but this is certain: England would topple headlong and carry the whole civilized world with her, save the South. No, you dare not make war on cotton. No power on earth dares to make war upon it. Cotton is king."

—James Henry Hammond, U.S. senator from South Carolina, March 4, 1858

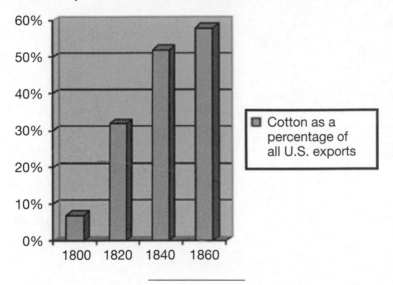

Based on this excerpt, Hammond believed
a. **cotton was becoming less important to the U.S. economy.**
b. **the Southern states had no chance of winning a civil war.**
c. **a cotton embargo was the best way to avoid civil war.**
d. **European countries would defend their ability to obtain cotton from the South.**

Answer: d. Southern strategy was based on the supposition that the country you threaten to blackmail will eventually come to your aid.

What modern example is similar to the South's position regarding cotton during the Civil War?
a. the United States and wheat
b. Greenland and ice
c. OPEC and oil
d. The United Nations and health care

· ·

Use the cartoon to answer the following two questions.

(The caption of this cartoon reads, *The Constitution gives the Negro the right to vote—but what care we for the Constitution.*)

What is the main idea represented by this political cartoon?
a. Southern whites did not think voting was important.
b. Southern whites kept African Americans from voting.
c. The national government protected African Americans who wanted to vote.
d. Slaves had trouble voting in the 1840s in the Deep South.

· ·

Answer: c. OPEC stands for the Organization of Petroleum Exporting Countries. This group attempted (and attempts) to use the availability and price of oil to control world politics, most notably regarding Middle Eastern politics. Oil is the closest late-twentieth-century equivalent to cotton production in the early/mid-1800s.

· ·

_____

Answer: b. The cartoon depicts a courageous, handsome, and unarmed African-American male attempting to vote. An angry-looking group of scraggly whites, including two wearing hoods to hide their identity, confronts him. The group is preventing the man from reaching the polls.

· ·

Based on the political cartoon, which 1960s law would probably be most important to the cartoonist?
a. Civil Rights Act
b. Voting Rights Act
c. Nationality and Immigration Act
d. Freedom of Information Act

. . . .

Use the passage to answer the following question.

We meet in the midst of a nation brought to the verge of moral, political, and material ruin. Corruption dominates the ballot box, the legislatures, the Congress, and touches even the ermine of the bench. The people are demoralized. . . . The newspapers are largely subsidized or muzzled; public opinion silenced; business prostrated; our homes covered with mortgages; labor impoverished; and land concentrating in the hands of capitalists. The urban workmen are denied the right of organization for self-protection. . . . The fruits of the toil of millions are boldly stolen to build up colossal fortunes for a few, unprecedented in the history of mankind; and the possessors of those, in turn, despise the republic and endanger liberty.
—"Populist Party Principles" from the "Omaha Platform," 1892

Which of the following does NOT deal with one of the issues addressed by the Populists?
a. the institution of a national income tax
b. the prohibition of alcohol
c. the power of unions
d. foreign affairs and the war in Europe

. . . .

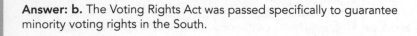

Answer: b. The Voting Rights Act was passed specifically to guarantee minority voting rights in the South.

· ·

_____

Answer: d. This ringing primary source excerpt is from the platform of the Populist Party, an important third party of the Gilded Age. Although unsuccessful at the ballot box, many of its ideas eventually were adopted by the Republican and Democratic parties. The Populists (and the early Progressives) were generally disinterested in foreign policy.

· ·

Answer the question based on the following excerpt from Babbitt, by Sinclair Lewis.

Just as he was an Elk, a Booster, and a member of the Chamber of Commerce, just as the priests of the Presbyterian Church determined his every religious belief and the senators who controlled the Republican Party decided in little smoky rooms in Washington what he should think about disarmament, tariff, and Germany, so did the large national advertisers fix the surface of his life, fix what he believed to be his individuality. These standard advertised wares—toothpastes, socks, tires, cameras, instantaneous hot-water heaters—were his symbols and proofs of excellence; at first the signs, then the substitutes, for joy and passion and wisdom.

——————

Which aspect of American life is NOT one of Sinclair Lewis's targets in this passage from Babbitt?
a. **American democracy**
b. **American foreign policy**
c. **American conformity**
d. **American consumerism**

_____

Answer: b. Although Lewis mentions disarmament, tariff, and Germany, he does not specifically say these policies are incorrect.

· ·

What is the best conclusion based on these two songs?

"I Didn't Raise My Boy to Be a Soldier" (1915)

Lyrics by Al Bryan, music by Al Piantadosi

"I didn't raise my boy to be a soldier, I brought him up to be my pride and joy. Who dares to place a musket on his shoulder To shoot some other mother's darling boy? Let nations arbitrate their future troubles, It's time to lay the sword and gun away; There'd be no war today if mothers would all say, 'I didn't raise my boy to be a soldier.'"

"Over There" (1917)

Music and Lyrics by George M. Cohan

Johnnie get your gun, get your gun, get your gun. Take it on the run, on the run, on the run. Hear them calling you and me, every son of liberty; Hurry right away, no delay, go today. Make your daddy glad to have had such a lad. Tell your sweetheart not to pine; to be proud her boy's in line.

a. **Americans were proud to have their children join World War I.**
b. **American soldiers in World War I fought for liberty.**
c. **Most Americans believed World War I was unnecessary.**
d. **Americans had different opinions about World War I.**

. . . .

Answer: d. The two songs take opposed views as to the value of enlisting and fighting in World War I.

· ·

Which is the best conclusion that can be drawn from the information below?

"Economic depression cannot be cured by legislative action or executive pronouncement. Economic wounds must be healed by the action of the cells of the economic body—the producers and consumers themselves. . . . The best contribution of government lies in encouragement of this voluntary cooperation in the community. The government—national, state, and local—can join with the community in such programs and do its part."
—President Herbert Hoover, Annual Message to the Congress on the State of the Union, Dec. 2, 1930

United States Government Finances, 1929–1941 (in Billions of Dollars)

Fiscal Year	Expenditures	Surplus or Deficit	Total Public Debt
1929	$3.127	$0.734	$16.9
1930	3.320	0.738	16.2
1931	3.577	−0.462	16.8
1932	4.659	−2.735	19.5
1933	4.598	−2.602	22.5
1934	6.645	−3.630	27.1
1935	6.497	−2.791	28.7
1936	8.422	−4.425	33.8
1937	7.733	−2.777	36.4
1938	6.765	−1.177	37.2
1939	8.841	−3.862	40.4
1940	9.589	−2.710	43.0
1941	13.980	−4.778	44.0

a. **Deficit spending contributed to increasing public debt in the 1930s.**
b. **The federal government should not be allowed to have deficit spending.**
c. **The public debt grew despite annual surpluses in the government's treasury.**
d. **The downward economic spiral was resolved only through significant expenditures of the federal government.**

. . . .

Answer: a. The government had a deficit from 1931 to 1941, which contributed to its debt.

Which conclusion can fairly be drawn from the graphic?

Population of Top Ten U.S. Cities in 1790

Rank	City
1	Philadelphia, PA
2	New York, NY
3	Boston, MA
4	Charleston, SC
5	Baltimore, MD
6	Salem, MA
7	Newport, RI
8	Providence, RI
9	Marblehead, MA
10	Portsmouth, NH

a. Southern cities had grown faster than Northern cities in the eighteenth century.
b. Immigrants were attracted to the largest cities in the newly formed United States.
c. Access to ports contributed to the growth of U.S. cities in the eighteenth century.
d. The Proclamation of 1763 prevented Americans from moving West in the newly formed United States.

Answer: c. The largest cities were port cities.

···

Use this passage to answer the following question.

President Lyndon Johnson is known for his efforts in fostering The Great Society. He instigated many U.S. programs focused on social reforms; however, some believed that his foreign policy conflicted with his goals at home. Military personnel from the United States were already stationed in Vietnam when Johnson came to the presidency, and U.S. involvement in the Vietnam War gave rise to great controversy.

During the Vietnam War, the total death toll exceeded 2 million, including approximately 58,000 Americans. In 1963, shortly after becoming U.S. president, Lyndon Johnson said, "I will not lose in Vietnam." In 1966, Johnson said, "I know we oughtn't to be there, but I can't get out . . . I just can't be the architect of surrender." Johnson's presidency ended in 1969. In 1973, under the presidency of Richard Nixon, U.S. troops were withdrawn from Vietnam.

Based on the evidence in this passage, which claim can reasonably be made?
a. Johnson's Great Society gave rise to his position regarding the Vietnam War.
b. Johnson was working to figure out a way for the United States to surrender in Vietnam.
c. Johnson's outlook regarding the Vietnam War changed as the years passed.
d. Johnson believed that architecture of buildings in Vietnam was important to the United States.

Answer: c. In 1963, Johnson makes this bold statement: "I will not lose in Vietnam." By 1966, however, Johnson states: "I know we oughtn't be there." This shows that his outlook has changed. He is commenting on the need to get out, rather than boldly stating that he will not lose.

Use the excerpt below, from the U.S. Supreme Court decision *Brown v. Board of Education* (1954), to answer the following question.

Where a State has undertaken to provide an opportunity for an education in its public schools, such an opportunity is a right which must be made available to all on equal terms. . . . Segregation of children in public schools solely on the basis of race deprives children of the minority group of equal educational opportunities, even though the physical facilities and other "tangible" factors may be equal. . . .

The legal doctrine struck down by the decision in *Brown v. the Board of Education* was the
a. **separate but equal doctrine**
b. **right to be made available doctrine**
c. **physical and tangible doctrine**
d. **public school or minority group doctrine**

_____

Answer: a. The excerpt states that segregation solely on the basis of race deprives children of equal educational opportunities. Segregated facilities are separate facilities, and the excerpt makes it clear that even though physical facilities may be equal, students are still deprived of equal opportunities when separation through segregation exists.

· ·

Use the excerpt below, from Abraham Lincoln's Gettysburg Address (1863), to answer the following question.

Four score and seven years ago our fathers brought forth, upon this continent, a new nation, conceived in liberty, and dedicated to the proposition that "all men are created equal."

Now we are engaged in a great civil war, testing whether that nation, or any nation so conceived, and so dedicated, can long endure. We are met on a great battle field of that war. We have come to dedicate a portion of it, as a final resting place for those who died here, that the nation might live. This we may, in all propriety do. But, in a larger sense, we can not dedicate—we can not consecrate—we can not hallow, this ground—The brave men, living and dead, who struggled here, have hallowed it, far above our poor power to add or detract. The world will little note, nor long remember what we say here; while it can never forget what they did here. . . .

_____

Abraham Lincoln begins the Gettysburg Address by referencing 1776, a pivotal year in American history, through "four score and seven years ago." The word *score* means a group or set of how many years?

a. 5

b. 10

c. 15

d. 20

. . . .

Answer: d. Noting the year of the Gettysburg Address, 1863, is important in determining the answer to this question. The question explains that Lincoln is referencing 1776, so:

$4 \times 20 = 80$

$80 + 7 = 87$

1863 (the year of the Gettysburg Address) − 87 = 1776.

. . . .

Use the information and timeline below, which depicts significant dates related to African-American Voting Rights in the United States, to answer the following three questions.

African-Americans
Voting Rights in the United States

1866
The U.S. Civil Rights Bill of 1866 grants citizenship to ex-slaves.

1868
The 14th Amendment to the U.S. Constitution becomes law.

1870
The 15th Amendment to the U.S. Constitution becomes law.

1915
Guinn v. United States, a U.S. Supreme Court decision, states that grandfather clauses are illegal because they violate the Fifteenth Amendment. (Grandfather clauses were developed to exempt whites from literacy tests, which had become a requirement for voting.)

1957
The Civil Rights Act of 1957 becomes law. It provides for a Commission on Civil Rights, and it establishes the power of the United States Attorney General to pursue remedies in court to enforce voting laws.

1964
The 24th Amendment to the U.S. Constitution becomes law.

Excerpt from the 14th Amendment to the United States Constitution
All persons born or naturalized in the United States, and subject to the jurisdiction thereof, are citizens of the United States and of the state wherein they reside. No state shall make or enforce any law which shall abridge the privileges or immunities of citizens of the United States; nor shall any state deprive any person of life, liberty, or property, without due process of law; nor deny to any person within its jurisdiction the equal protection of the laws. . . .

Excerpt from the 15th Amendment to the United States Constitution
The right of citizens of the United States to vote shall not be denied or abridged by the United States or by any state on account of race, color, or previous condition of servitude. . . .

Excerpt from the 24th Amendment to the United States Constitution
The right of citizens of the United States to vote in any primary or other election for President or Vice President, for electors for President or Vice President, or for Senator or Representative in Congress, shall not be denied or abridged by the United States or any state by reason of failure to pay any poll tax or other tax. . . .

Based on the information provided, which best states the relationship between the 1866 U.S. Civil Rights Bill and the amendments shown?
a. The 1866 U.S. Civil Rights Bill was relatively unimportant to the development of the Twenty-Fourth Amendment.
b. The amendments would not have applied to African Americans if they had not been determined to be citizens.
c. The Fourteenth and Fifteenth Amendments were major contributors to the development of civil rights legislation prior to 1950.
d. The Fifteenth Amendment is not related in any way, but the Fourteenth Amendment and the 1866 U.S. Civil Rights Bill are related.

. . . .

Place the following events in the correct chronological order, from earliest to latest.
I. Civil Rights Act of 1957
II. 15th Amendment
III. *Guinn* v. *United States*
IV. Civil Rights Bill of 1866
a. I, II, III, IV
b. II, I, III, IV
c. IV, II, III, I
d. III, IV, I, II

. . . .

Based on the information provided, which conclusion regarding voting after 1964 by African Americans in the United States is logical?
a. It decreased.
b. It remained about the same.
c. It increased.
d. It stopped abruptly.

Answer: b. The amendments apply to citizens; without the status of citizens, African Americans would not have been entitled to these rights.

. . . .

Answer: c. This is the correct chronological sequence of events.

. . . .

Answer: c. All of the identified events are related to legislative and judicial strides in voting rights for African Americans. It is logical to conclude that after all these strides had been made, substantially more African Americans would have the right to vote and would utilize this right.

SUGAR ALLOWANCE COUPON

1 Pound — For Home Food Processing — **1 Pound**

OPA Form No. R-327

This coupon authorizes the holder to whom it was issued to receive 1 pound of sugar, which is to be used only to conserve fruit, fruit juices, or other foods as specified in the Regulations for the use of the person or persons listed on the Home Canning Sugar Application (Form No. R-323) or the Special Purpose Application (Form No. R-315) on file at the office of the Board indicated below.

Serial Number of War Ration Book ....

Board No. .... State ....

☆ GPO 16—33320-1

Accessed through Northwestern University Library
https://images.northwestern.edu/multiresimages/
inu:dil-356cd140-0ef0-4695-90db-052d542a9dc2

These types of stamps were common during World War II, as many items were rationed. Based on the image, what is the best definition of the word *ration*, as used on the stamp?

a. "preferred quota"
b. "fixed amount"
c. "passage fare"
d. "acceleration scale"

―――――――――

Answer: b. The ration is the fixed amount people were entitled to obtain.

· ·

Use the excerpt below to answer the following question.

The 5th Amendment to the U.S. Constitution

No person shall be held to answer for a capital, or otherwise infamous crime, unless on a presentment or indictment of a grand jury, except in cases arising in the land or naval forces, or in the militia, when in actual service in time of war or public danger; nor shall any person be subject for the same offense to be twice put in jeopardy of life or limb; nor shall be compelled in any criminal case to be a witness against himself, nor be deprived of life, liberty, or property, without due process of law; nor shall private property be taken for public use, without just compensation.

When a person has been charged with a crime and claims due process rights, refusing to testify, this relates most closely to which part of the Fifth Amendment?

a. **No person shall be held to answer for a capital, or otherwise infamous crime, unless on a presentment or indictment of a grand jury**

b. **nor shall any person be subject for the same offense to be twice put in jeopardy of life or limb**

c. **nor shall be compelled in any criminal case to be a witness against himself, nor be deprived of life, liberty, or property, without due process of law**

d. **nor shall private property be taken for public use, without just compensation**

_____

Answer: c. A defendant in a criminal case may decide not to testify in the case. This is the legal right of the defendant.

Use the excerpts below, taken from the inaugural addresses of President Barack Obama, to answer the following two questions. Note that President Obama references many issues, including the economy and war in the Middle East.

Excerpt from President Barack Obama's Inaugural Address, 2009
That we are in the midst of crisis is now well understood. Our nation is at war against a far-reaching network of violence and hatred. Our economy is badly weakened, a consequence of greed and irresponsibility on the part of some but also our collective failure to make hard choices and prepare the nation for a new age.

Homes have been lost, jobs shed, businesses shuttered. Our health care is too costly, our schools fail too many, and each day brings further evidence that the ways we use energy strengthen our adversaries and threaten our planet . . .

Excerpt from President Barack Obama's Inaugural Address, 2013
This generation of Americans has been tested by crises that steeled our resolve and proved our resilience. A decade of war is now ending. An economic recovery has begun. America's possibilities are limitless, for we possess all the qualities that this world without boundaries demands: youth and drive; diversity and openness; an endless capacity for risk and a gift for reinvention. My fellow Americans, we are made for this moment, and we will seize it—so long as we seize it together . . .

In these two inaugural addresses, some statements express optimism, while others do not. Which of these statements expresses the greatest optimism?
a. That we are in the midst of crisis is now well understood.
b. Our nation is at war against a far-reaching network of violence and hatred.
c. This generation of Americans has been tested by crises that steeled our resolve and proved our resilience.
d. America's possibilities are limitless, for we possess all the qualities that this world without boundaries demands: youth and drive; diversity and openness; an endless capacity for risk and a gift for reinvention.

Answer: d. After events during President Obama's first term in office, he expressed great optimism in this excerpt from the second address. Phrases such as "possibilities are limitless" and "endless capacity" provide guides to recognize Obama's optimism.

In 2009, Obama stated: "A decade of war is now ending." Select the part of the world where this war had been fought.
a. Africa (sub-Sahara)
b. East Asia and the Pacific
c. Middle East
d. South and Central Asia

. . . .

Answer: c. The introduction to the excerpt explains that President Obama referenced the war in Iraq, which is located in the Middle East.

· ·

Use the information below to answer the following question.

During the 1950s and 1960s, a space race developed between the United States and the Soviets. The Soviets launched *Sputnik* in 1957. It was the first satellite launched into space. Implications of potential impact on the Cold War and the conflict between democracy and communism became clear. The United States forged ahead to take its place in the space race.

"First, I believe that this nation should commit itself to achieving the goal, before this decade is out, of landing a man on the moon and returning him safely to the earth. . . . "

—President John F. Kennedy
Special Message to the Congress on Urgent National Needs
May 25, 1961

"That's one small step for a man, one giant leap for mankind."
—Neil Armstrong from the surface of the moon
July 16, 1969

"Yes, I thought about it after landing, and because we had a lot of other things to do, it was not something that I really concentrated on but just something that was kind of passing around subliminally or in the background. But it, you know, was a pretty simple statement, talking about stepping off something. Why, it wasn't a very complex thing. It was what it was."

Neil Armstrong
Interview in Houston, Texas, when asked about the statement
"That's one small step for a man, one giant leap for mankind."
September 19, 2001

_____

Which statement accurately describes the relationship among events and the three quotes?
a. **Armstrong carefully crafted the statement for his first step on the moon.**
b. **The United States urgently needed materials from other planets.**
c. **Armstrong planned to explore Earth for humankind.**
d. **President Kennedy's goal was realized.**

———————

Answer: d. In 1961, President Kennedy stated that his goal was to put a man on the moon and return him safely to Earth. In 1969, before the decade had ended, Neil Armstrong had set foot on the moon, and as Armstrong was interviewed in 2001, it is clear that he returned safely to Earth.

Use the excerpts below, taken from the Constitution of the United States and the First Amendment to the Constitution of the United States, to answer the following two questions.

The Constitution of the United States (1787)
We the People of the United States, in Order to form a more perfect Union, establish Justice, insure domestic Tranquility, provide for the common defence, promote the general Welfare, and secure the Blessings of Liberty to ourselves and our Posterity, do ordain and establish this Constitution for the United States of America.

Article I. Section. 1. All legislative Powers herein granted shall be vested in a Congress of the United States, which shall consist of a Senate and House of Representatives.

Amendment I (1791)
Congress shall make no law respecting an establishment of religion, or prohibiting the free exercise thereof; or abridging the freedom of speech, or of the press; or the right of the people peaceably to assemble, and to petition the Government for a redress of grievances.

These excerpts are taken from the public domain.

_____

Based on the excerpts, which of the following has the right to establish laws to insure [ensure] domestic tranquility, provide for the common defence [defense], and promote the general welfare of and for people in the United States?
a. unions in the United States
b. Congress of the United States
c. citizens of the United States
d. Supreme Court Justices in the United States

———————————

Answer: b. Article I states that legislative powers, which are powers to make laws, are vested in Congress.

Based on information in the excerpts, which statement can be clearly inferred?

a. Article I, Section 1 of the Constitution is not as important as the First Amendment to the Constitution.

b. Amendments, including the First Amendment, were needed to address issues that were not specifically addressed in the Constitution.

c. The Constitution was initially written to provide individual rights and liberties; however, the First Amendment did not address individual rights and liberties.

d. From a historical perspective, it appears that the First Amendment was an afterthought of lawmakers in the United States and was not considered to be of great significance.

. . . .

Answer: b. It is clear that the First Amendment addresses issues that are not specifically addressed in the Constitution.

· ·

Use the excerpt and quote below to answer the following two questions.

Emancipation Proclamation
January 1, 1863

By the President of the United States of America:

A Proclamation.

Whereas, on the twenty-second day of September, in the year of our Lord one thousand eight hundred and sixty-two, a proclamation was issued by the President of the United States, containing, among other things, the following, to wit:

That on the first day of January, in the year of our Lord one thousand eight hundred and sixty-three, all persons held as slaves within any State or designated part of a State, the people whereof shall then be in rebellion against the United States, shall be then, thenceforward, and forever free; and the Executive Government of the United States, including the military and naval authority thereof, will recognize and maintain the freedom of such persons, and will do no act or acts to repress such persons, or any of them, in any efforts they may make for their actual freedom. . . .

By the President: ABRAHAM LINCOLN
WILLIAM H. SEWARD, Secretary of State.

"Until justice is blind to color, until education is unaware of race, until opportunity is unconcerned with the color of men's skins, emancipation will be a proclamation but not a fact. To the extent that the proclamation of emancipation is not fulfilled in fact, to that extent we shall have fallen short of assuring freedom to the free . . . "

—President Lyndon B. Johnson
Gettysburg, Pennsylvania
May 30, 1963

As used in the passage, the two words that have almost the same meaning are
a. *proclamation* and *rebellion*
b. *repress* and *maintain*
c. *freedom* and *emancipation*
d. *military* and *rebellion*

———————

Answer: c. The slaves' freedom and their emancipation are the same. A proclamation is an official statement, and a rebellion is an open resistance to an existing government. To repress is to subdue or restrain, and to maintain is to allow a condition to continue. While repression of slaves would have meant maintaining the existing conditions, repressing and maintaining are not synonymous.

• •

Based on the excerpts, which statement regarding the viewpoints of Lincoln and Johnson is accurate?

a. Johnson's statements indicate that he believed in the philosophy of Lincoln's emancipation proclamation, but that more work toward emancipation needed to be done.

b. While Lincoln was in favor of emancipation of slaves, Johnson opposed emancipation of slaves.

c. Lincoln's statements in the Emancipation Proclamation were based on analysis of Johnson's statements.

d. While Johnson believed that justice should be blind to color, Lincoln believed that color was important in determining justice.

· ·

Answer: a. Johnson's initial statements provide evidence to show that he believes that opportunities should be available, regardless of skin color; this indicates that he agrees with Lincoln. Johnson also states that people have fallen short of assuring freedom to the free, which provides evidence to show that he believes more work needs to be done.

Use the excerpts below to answer the following three questions.

The U.S. Supreme Court decision *Plessy v. Ferguson* (1896) focused on a man described as "of mixed descent, in the proportion of seven-eighths Caucasian and one-eighth African blood; that the mixture of colored blood was not discernible in him . . . " The man boarded a train in Louisiana and sat in "a vacant seat in a coach where passengers of the white race were accommodated . . . " When asked to move to a different location on the train, a location designated for "persons not of the white race," the man refused. A police officer forcibly removed him from the train, and the man was charged with a crime.

Majority Opinion, delivered by Justice Brown

. . . 2. By the fourteenth amendment, all persons born or naturalized in the United States, and subject to the jurisdiction thereof, are made citizens of the United States and of the state wherein they reside; and the states are forbidden from making or enforcing any law which shall abridge the privileges or immunities of citizens of the United States, or shall deprive any person of life, liberty, or property without due process of law, or deny to any person within their jurisdiction the equal protection of the laws.

So far, then, as a conflict with the fourteenth amendment is concerned, the case reduces itself to the question whether the statute [law] of Louisiana is a reasonable regulation, and with respect to this there must necessarily be a large discretion on the part of the legislature. In determining the question of reasonableness, it is at liberty to act with reference to the established usages, customs, and traditions of the people, and with a view to the promotion of their comfort, and the preservation of the public peace and good order. Gauged by this standard, we cannot say that a law which authorizes or even requires the separation of the two races in public conveyances . . . is unreasonable, or more obnoxious to the fourteenth amendment than the acts of congress requiring separate schools for colored children in the District of Columbia, the constitutionality of which does not seem to have been questioned, or the corresponding acts of state legislatures.

GED® TEST SOCIAL STUDIES FLASH REVIEW

Dissent by Justice Harlan

. . . If evils will result from the commingling of the two races upon public highways established for the benefit of all, they will be infinitely less than those that will surely come from state legislation regulating the enjoyment of civil rights upon the basis of race. We boast of the freedom enjoyed by our people above all other peoples. But it is difficult to reconcile that boast with a state of the law which, practically, puts the brand of servitude and degradation upon a large class of our fellow citizens,-our equals before the law. The thin disguise of 'equal' accommodations for passengers in railroad coaches will not mislead any one, nor atone for the wrong this day done . . .

I am of opinion that the state of Louisiana is inconsistent with the personal liberty of citizens, white and black, in that state, and hostile to both the spirit and letter of the constitution of the United States . . . Slavery, as an institution tolerated by law, would, it is true, have disappeared from our country; but there would remain a power in the states, by sinister legislation, to interfere with the full enjoyment of the blessings of freedom, to regulate civil rights, common to all citizens, upon the basis of race, and to place in a condition of legal inferiority a large body of American citizens . . .

In his dissent, Justice Harlan compares the results of the majority opinion to what?
a. some blessings of freedom
b. established usages, customs, and traditions of the people
c. a brand of servitude and degradation
d. the personal liberty of citizens, white and black

· ·

The opinion that reflects the law of the present day is the opinion of Justice _____.

· ·

Which best states the meaning of *institution* in the excerpt?
a. beginning
b. practice
c. society
d. university

GED® TEST SOCIAL STUDIES FLASH REVIEW

Answer: c. Harlan references the law made by the majority opinion when he states that it is difficult to reconcile the boast of freedom for people with the state of the law that puts a brand of servitude and degradation upon fellow citizens. While Harlan does reference blessings of freedom, he does not reference blessings of freedom as resulting from the majority opinion. While Harlan references the personal liberty of citizens, white and black, he does not state that this liberty is a result of the majority opinion. Established usages, customs, and traditions of the people are referenced in the majority opinion, not Harlan's dissent.

· ·

Answer: Harlan. Harlan believes that separate facilities are not equal facilities. The decision in *Plessy v. Ferguson* was later struck down by the Supreme Court when the court held that separate facilities are not equal facilities; this later decision correlates to Justice Harlan's dissenting opinion.

· ·

Answer: b. The excerpt states the following: "Slavery, as an institution tolerated by law, would, it is true, have disappeared from our country. . . ." The excerpt is referencing the practice of slavery being tolerated.

Use the excerpts below to answer the following question.

Franklin Roosevelt's Statement on Signing the Social Security Act (1935)

Today a hope of many years' standing is in large part fulfilled. The civilization of the past hundred years, with its startling industrial changes, has tended more and more to make life insecure. Young people have come to wonder what would be their lot when they came to old age. The man with a job has wondered how long the job would last.

This social security measure gives at least some protection to thirty million of our citizens who will reap direct benefits through unemployment compensation, through old-age pensions and through increased services for the protection of children and the prevention of ill health.

We can never insure one hundred percent of the population against one hundred percent of the hazards and vicissitudes of life, but we have tried to frame a law which will give some measure of protection to the average citizen and to his family against the loss of a job and against poverty-ridden old age. . . .

"Should any political party attempt to abolish social security, unemployment insurance, and eliminate labor laws and farm programs, you would not hear of that party again in our political history."

—Dwight D. Eisenhower
written in a letter to his brother
1954

—————————

As expressed in the speech excerpt and statement from Eisenhower, how do the viewpoints of Roosevelt and Eisenhower regarding social security compare?

a. **Neither has a strong opinion regarding social security.**
b. **Both believe in the importance of social security in the country.**
c. **Neither thinks social security will survive into the future.**
d. **Both anticipate constitutional amendments to strengthen social security.**

Answer: b. Roosevelt speaks of the hope and protection provided by social security. Eisenhower states that a political party attempting to abolish social security would essentially disappear from the political landscape.